Praise for The Butcher, The Baker, The Candlestick Maker

'It was so hot, I just wanted to stop reading and have sex,'
Cosmopolitan

'For once an author has got it right . . . Book of the Month,'
Scarlet

'Ravenous, sexually charged,' *Men's Health*

'Intelligently written (and) brutally honest,' *Metro*

'Eye-poppingly unambiguous prose,' *Esquire*

'Gritty and Explicit,' *The Observer*

'As mind-boggling as it is shocking,' *The Mirror*

'The woman who has it all has it off,' *Word Magazine*

'Breathy and explicit,' *The Jewish Chronicle*

Other books by Suzanne Portnoy

The Not So Invisible Woman

THE BUTCHER, THE BAKER, THE CANDLESTICK MAKER

Suzanne Portnoy

This paperback edition published in 2008 by
Virgin Books Ltd
Thames Wharf Studios
Rainville Road
London W6 9HA

First published in Great Britain in 2006 by Virgin Books Ltd

A catalogue record of this book is available from the
British Library

Distributed in the USA by Holtzbrinck Publishers, LLC,
175 Fifth Avenue, New York, NY 10010, USA

The Random House Group Limited supports The Forest
Stewardship Council [FSC], the leading international forest
certification organisation. All our titles that are printed on
Greenpeace approved FSC certified paper carry the FSC logo
Our paper procurement policy can be found at
www.rbooks.co.uk/environment

Mixed Sources
Product group from well-managed
forests and other controlled sources
www.fsc.org Cert no. TT-COC-002227
© 1996 Forest Stewardship Council

FSC

ISBN 978 0 7535 1101 5

Typeset by Phoenix Photosetting, Chatham, Kent
Printed and bound in Great Britain by
CPI Bookmarque, Croydon, Surrey

1 3 5 7 9 10 8 6 4 2

ACKNOWLEDGEMENTS

To Michael O'Loughlin, collaborator, editor, friend, who made this book possible.

To Adam Nevill at Virgin Books, who believed in me and supported me from the start.

To my parents, who taught me the most important thing in life is my own happiness.

To my children, who love me despite my being an unconventional mother.

To Tony Semerad, the first guy to make me come, and to all the men who followed – thanks for the memories, guys.

To Geri, who listened to my stories, laughed, and never judged.

To CP, who set me on my journey.

Some names and situations have been changed to protect identities.

The author is aware that the websites and newspapers mentioned did not and could not control her interaction with members.

Awakening is not something newly discovered; it has always existed. There is no need to seek or follow the advice of others. Learn to listen to that voice within yourself just here and now. Your body and mind will become clear and you will realise the unity of all things. Do not doubt the possibilities because of the simplicity of these teachings. If you can't find the truth right where you are, where else do you think you will find it?

– Buddhist Text

Is that a gun in your pocket, or are you just glad to see me?

– Mae West

1. AN APERITIF AT RIO'S

Mr New York, Action Man, the Scottish Antonio Banderas, the French Gigolo, the Danish Pastry, Tantric Andy, Opera Man, and on and on. And on. I rarely call them by their names. My friend Michelle says my men shouldn't get a name until I've slept with them three times and, using her criteria, most of them remain nameless. That doesn't bother me. I'm not looking for a boyfriend. I'm looking for sex. It's my weekend retreat.

That's where Rio's comes in.

My kids-free weekends always start with me in the car. There's the rush out of my office at five-thirty p.m., the zigzag through the Hampstead back streets to avoid the rush-hour traffic, and the quick hello to the kids, who are usually so immersed in the latest PlayStation game they barely notice my greeting. I yank clothes out of the laundry basket, making sure I've got enough tops, pants and pyjamas, adding something heavy for a sudden cold snap and something light for a rare

British heatwave. I got divorced almost five years ago and my kids still don't keep any clothes with my ex, so we operate on a rotating wardrobe scheme whereby every other week, when my ex has the kids, I ferry a bag of stuff over to his spotless penthouse flat, which he will later wash and return to me on Sunday when I collect the kids.

Weekends start off well if I've got the kids in the car by six-thirty and over to their father a few minutes later. If I make it to Rio's by seven, I get fucked for free. Otherwise, the admission fee kicks in, and I'm paying £11 for the privilege of getting laid. Until Sunday evening, when I cross London again to pick up my sons, it's 'me' time.

Many Friday evenings I'm tempted to stay home, pour a glass of wine and put my feet up, rather than serve as a human shuttle service. It's a struggle to get ready to go out on the town. I'm tired after a busy work week. My super king-size bed is calling, calling, even if I'll be jumping into it alone. And yet I think, Stop being so pathetic. You've just turned forty-four, for fuck's sake, and there are many men out there. And I've only got four days and two nights a month to meet them. When my ex-husband has custody, I have my freedom. And freedom means sex.

The temptation to stay home is short-lived tonight, bested by the temptations to be found at Rio's and the opportunity to be seduced by an anonymous male and serviced by him. I've got a web date and although, as usual for a Friday, part of me wants to take the easy option and send him a text to call the whole thing off, I can't. My date has travelled from Winchester to see me. Calling it off so late, and after his two-and-a-half-hour drive, would be rude. I was brought up to be a good girl.

His picture and his profile on TotallyGorgeous.com look pretty good. His photo shows off his fair hair and broad shoulders. He is wearing a blue Lacoste shirt – public-schoolboy vanilla – but he looks tall and athletic and his broad shoulders stretch the cotton at the collar and sleeve. Nice. Not as 'totally gorgeous' as the site's name promises, not a super-model, but good enough for one evening. He said he works in finance, which, since he lives too far south to work in the City, makes me wonder if he sells pension plans: boring.

'What are you into?' he asked, after a few email exchanges, when we spoke on the phone. 'Do you ever go out clubbing?'

I told him I went to fetish clubs from time to time, and that excited him. He actually gasped, which made me wonder just how extensive a sexual history someone in a Lacoste shirt really had. I always get worried when guys think going to a fetish club is the height of decadence. Anyone who's ever spent ten minutes in Torture Garden knows these places are costume parties for grown-ups. There's always the same middle-aged man in chaps being spanked by his overweight dominatrix partner, while hotties hover on the periphery, watching the show.

'I wouldn't mind being your companion at a fetish club if you're ever short of a date,' Mr Lacoste had said. He seemed disappointed when I told him I had a regular partner for fetish-club nights, but we agreed to get together anyway.

The only other guy I've met on TotallyGorgeous was also in finance – a banker with a penchant for talking dirty but who had bipolar disorder. Halfway through a blowjob he said to me, in his upper-crust English accent, 'You know, I haven't had an orgasm in ten years.'

I took this as a challenge, the equivalent of climbing Mount Everest to make him come. I failed. He was on lithium. While I was on Everest, he was in the clouds. I got a nice steak frites from the banker, at least. Tonight I'm hoping for three courses and a sexual aperitif.

I'm not scheduled to meet the web date until ten p.m. and it's only six-thirty. I have three hours to kill. I'm coming back from my ex's and am stopped at a light at Tufnell Park Station. It's a nondescript part of north London, with a strip of fish-and-chip shops, Indian takeaways and a Sainsbury's Local. If I go straight, I'm on Dartmouth Park Road, heading home, where I'll wait for my date. If I turn left, I'm on the

Kentish Town Road, headed to Rio's. I'm reminded of John, the killer in Luke Rhinehart's novel *Dice Man*, who shakes the die at night and, depending on how they fall, either goes out in search of a victim or stays at home with a hot pot of tea. I play my own version of the game: if there's a parking space in front of Rio's, I'll go in; no space, and I'll go home. Two minutes later I spot a space directly in front. That's the sign I'm looking for.

There are only eight spaces in front of Rio's, so even in the off hours scoring one can be tricky. Regulars at this self-described naturist health-and-relaxation club say the local Council changed the nearby Pay and Display machine from all day to two hours maximum, because Rio's' many customers monopolised the few spaces on the high street. I've met people who've stayed at Rio's from when it opened at eleven a.m. until it closed at seven a.m. the following day. They grumble about having to run outside in their towels to deposit coins in the parking machine.

'Fucking Camden Council. They really know how to take the fun out of life,' said one man I was fondling in the Jacuzzi, who lost his rod when he realised he had five minutes left on his parking voucher.

I turn the white plastic handle on the front door and enter Rio's reception. The space is designed to fit about five people and its décor is minimal: a wicker chair in one corner and a mural on one wall featuring a topless woman in a sarong reclining on a beach in Polynesia. There's also a glass window through which customers receive their essential equipment – a fluffy white towel, which comes in handy later. I've never actually seen anyone sit on that chair, nor have I seen anyone wait in the reception area. Most people are anxious to get inside, where the action happens. The receptionist is in the back office beyond the glass window. She looks pissed off today, but then she always looks pissed off. As the dour and lumpy controlling finger on the buzzer, she's the one who witnesses my frequent comings and goings, and I always wonder if she's resentful, or even jealous, of the number of times she's buzzed me up to the 'relaxation rooms' reserved for couples or, in my case, singles with strangers. Maybe she wishes she were seeing that kind of action herself.

The new admission rate – free for girls Sunday to Friday, eleven a.m. to seven p.m. – is designed to attract more women, as that's what keeps the men paying £18 to get in. It's expensive to look at tits. I'm not sure they're getting what they pay for. Most of the women who come now insist on wearing their swimming costumes, denying men even the peep. Too many women treat Rio's like it's a trip to the hairdresser, spending most of their time in the steam room putting conditioner on their hair. Before the girls got in free – my heyday – it was rare to see a single woman at Rio's. Even then, women used the place as a kind of health-and-relaxation centre, and, even though that's what the brochure says it is, these girls blow the atmosphere. They are not there for the very thing Rio's is really devoted to: sex.

Because I tend to go during the day, I am a rarity. And, because I walk around naked, I'm as exotic as the Polynesian chick in the painting. And since so few women interface with the men, at least during the daylight hours, I've pretty much got this beach all to myself.

From the expressions I see on other women's faces, I can tell they think nudity is not so respectable. There is disapproval in their watchful eyes. None has ever commented, but they seem to perceive my nakedness as a transgression; whereas, given the sign over the front door advertises it as a naturist club, I feel they, too, should be naked. Might their discomfort arise from the disparity between the number of men and women? Men outnumber women by about ten to one at any time and, when I am there, only one woman is naked – me. Maybe they really do think of Rio's as a health club, and I'm the only one who gets fucked there. Or it could be that few other women have figured out that, if you're a naked woman in a room with ten naked men, some of whom are displaying some degree of arousal, it's easy to get laid.

In any case, I just like being naked. I'm not shy about my body. I'm a 5'5", blue-eyed blonde and, after investing years with a personal trainer, I'm finally down from a size 16 to my dream size, 12. I'm a busty 34DD, with a small waist, a woman's hips, a flat stomach and a round bottom. I reckon I've done about ten thousand lunges over the past ten years and have great legs to show for it. I'm not vain, but I do like being noticed. It has taken me forty-four years to look this good and feel confident about my appearance.

En route to the ladies' changing room after the receptionist has handed me my fluffy white towel, I glance at the lounging area to check out the talent. Rio's is a bit of a dive. It has no state-of-the-art equipment, no Philippe Starck-designed interior or, in fact, any design at all except for a tropical theme that would be sadly dated were it not so unintentionally ironic. But it's functional. And it delivers what I want: sex on tap.

Today there are a couple of average-looking guys crashed out on the cheap plastic loungers, staring at the wall. There are three rows of ten loungers here, each facing the wall-mounted television that permanently shows either football or soap operas, which strikes me as odd for a swingers club. The men glance at me. As always, there is at least one in whom I detect some interest. I ignore them all and move on to the changing room.

A large window separates the lounge area from the 'bar', which, instead of alcohol, serves orange squash, lemonade, water, coffee and tea, along with digestive biscuits for dunking, all free to customers. Those with a wholesome appetite may purchase toasted sandwiches. 'Nice touch,' said a boyfriend the first time he accompanied me to Rio's. 'A toastie between mouthfuls, as it were.'

Across the room I catch a glimpse of an old guy sitting on a bar stool. I would guess, based on his wrinkled torso and equally wrinkled face and the seven remaining strands of grey hair on his head, he must be about eighty years old. I recognise him from past visits, as he is a permanent fixture here, usually found at the bar, naked except for the towel wrapped around his sagging waist, chatting with the topless waitress with the bad tit job, colourful sarong and kinky Marigolds. I often wonder if the old guy owns the place, but I've never thought to ask. It could simply be Rio's is just happy for his £18.

I enter the changing room. There are rows of small yellow lockers on all four walls of the three-metres-square room. Green plastic outdoor chairs of the type normally found at barbecues sit in two of the corners, and a large blue plastic bucket for the used towels is in a third. I grab a plastic bracelet on which a key is fastened, turn it, and a locker pops open. I take off my clothes, wrap the towel around me, pop a £1 coin into the locker to release the key, and then fasten the bracelet to my wrist, taking a quick look at myself in the full-length mirror. I think I look pretty good, if not fucking hot. Well, not so fucking hot after all, because I see rings around my ankles, showing where the elastic of my socks pinched my skin, and another around my waist from my admittedly too-tight jeans. It's not a great look, but I know from experience that, after a few minutes in the steam room and Jacuzzi, the rings will disappear.

As I pass through the lounging area, I take a better look at the bodies on the loungers. There's a middle-aged Indian guy with a big belly passed out on one. A skinny young white guy with a complete absence of muscles is asleep on another. A short Greek man about fifty years old, a commercial airline pilot whom I've met before, is sitting on a third. He nods hello and returns to the football rerun. None of them takes my fancy, so I walk past them to the spa. There are two Jacuzzis on the right, each large enough for six people but now empty. A small steam room is on the left, and further ahead are two saunas and two more steam rooms. Through an archway further down the hall is a small swimming pool and a very large Jacuzzi that can hold about twenty but it is closed. Beyond that is the smoking area, which is usually empty, and past that two 'relaxation' rooms that often host orgies but that always reek of cigarettes, since smokers tend to combine one pleasure with another at this end of the hall. As a vehement anti-smoker, I never go this far down the hall. I indulge other vices.

I enter one of the saunas and see a good-looking fit black guy whom a year ago I fucked two Friday lunchtimes in a row. He's about thirty-five and is bald and muscular, with a great six-pack and a thick nine-inch cock. I definitely remember him, but he either hasn't seen me come in or is pretending he doesn't know me. This is suspect, because typically all heads turn when a new body enters a sauna; even those not on the lookout for fresh meat notice when cold air breaks the heat of a sauna.

Mr Familiar is rubbing the back of a black woman in a bikini. It's an intimate moment for the two of them, but I don't care. I stare at him alone. He continues not to look my way and part of me wonders whether I should interrupt their revelry and say hello, if only to send the message 'Fuck you for ignoring me.' Then I wonder if what I really want to say is 'Fuck you for not remembering me.' While contemplating this ego quagmire, I don't say anything, but I continue to stare at him and he continues to ignore me. Ultimately, I graciously decide now is not the appropriate moment to remind him that, just a year ago, we were each other's Friday lunchtime dish.

We really had connected on those two Fridays. The sex was great – great enough that he was the only Rio's man I'd ever arranged to meet a second time. It's possible that he truly did forget me. That's the way it goes in such places. If you sleep with enough people, after a while you lose track. The brain can only store so much information before it shunts memories into little compartments that eventually get buried under dust. Still, when his hands reach under his lady friend's string top, I feel a twinge of jealousy.

The sauna door opens. In walks another guy I've met before. This one's white, about forty and 5'10", slim and slightly muscular, with spiky dark-blond hair. He's tanned and quite handsome, with an angular face, beautiful eyes and high cheekbones – Ed Harris with hair. He takes off his towel and sits down next to me on the hot wooden bench. 'Hello,' he says. 'Haven't seen you here for a while. I'm John.'

For a few seconds I debate whether I want to talk to him. The last time we met, John was a major pain in the ass. Yet today I'm almost grateful that someone here remembers me. It's disconcerting to think you're a good fuck, and even be told you're one, and then not be remembered.

'No,' I respond. 'I haven't been here in a month or so.' I do not add, 'Nice to see you again.' Flattered, or relieved, as I am by his attention, I am weighing up whether I want to carry on the conversation. Rio's was meant to be just a pitstop. After all, I have a web date tonight, Mr Lacoste, and there's a strong chance, based on his sexy text messages and phone calls, I might end up taking him home after dinner.

I hadn't planned on coming to Rio's for anything more than a chill-out, but John is obviously coming on to me. How do I know this? He's naked and I can see his cock thickening, already eight inches even in a semi-aroused state. Nothing like a growing cock to indicate a man's interest.

What if my web date doesn't work out? I find myself wondering. Suddenly, like Dice Man, I have options. Should I (a) take what's on offer now and greedily anticipate a second round in a few hours, or (b) reject the here-and-now man and risk getting blown off by my dinner date? Web dates are notoriously unreliable, and I'm reminded that my one previous experience with a man from TotallyGorgeous was not a success. There's a fifty-fifty chance Mr Lacoste may turn out to be a loser – or, worse, a no-show. One thing is clear, however: not getting fucked at all is not an option. I love sex. My kids-free Friday nights come along just twice a month, and I have to take advantage of them.

'Do you fancy having a massage?' he asks. Massage is the code word for sex in this particular establishment.

'Sure,' I say. I have chosen option (a).

It's a good thing John's cock helps me to overlook his peculiarities. He and I have a history that makes me less than enthusiastic about spending much time with him. One time I had gone to Rio's with a guy named Andy, who'd advertised his services as a tantric masseur and stud. I'd begun exploring tantric as an alternative to the anonymous swinging scene, but the former hadn't yet replaced the latter, and I wanted our first meeting to be in a safe public space. Though not an ideal venue for a spiritual sexual encounter, Rio's certainly is public, so I suggested that Tantric Andy meet me there. He'd had some swinging experiences, anyway, having done his share of three-somes and gang bangs, so, despite his reservations about the place, he agreed to meet me at Rio's. Tantric Andy and I were in a Jacuzzi when John plunged into the water and sat down next to us. He kept staring at me, and at us as a couple. I got the impression from the way he kept glancing at my tits that he was more voyeur than bisexual. And then I felt his hand on my thigh.

I've met guys like him in Jacuzzis before – guys that start out stroking my leg and are soon rubbing my pussy while jerking themselves off. How far I let them go depends on how attractive I find them. Most times I remove their hand from my leg and that's where it ends.

At first, from the way his free hand was moving up and down beneath the surface of the water, it looked like John was jerking himself off while feeling my right thigh. Tantric Andy, meanwhile, had his hand on my left thigh. I found it erotic, the idea that John might be masturbating while looking at me and not knowing for sure if he was.

Then I felt John's hand move further up my leg, before stopping just inches from my pussy. I removed his hand. No words were spoken. Soon after, he put his hand on my leg again, and again I took it off – on and off, on and off. If I'd been alone or not on a first date, or if my date was not sitting next to me, I probably would have left John's hand there. If he'd been unattractive and kept at it, I probably would have twisted his wrist and maybe even reported him to the management for harassment. Rio's may seem like a sexual free-for-all, but, as with all clubs, there are rules, the most important being: 'Ask before you touch.'

John was pissing me off, so I suggested to Tantric Andy we leave and go back to mine. Andy had by then passed the test. He was sweet and kind of cute and, from what he had told me, he could give me a damn good massage. And then, of course, there was his not insubstantial cock that I'd casually stroked in the Jacuzzi for the purposes of research.

When we stepped out of the Jacuzzi, John followed us. He stood at the entrance to the showers, cock in hand, stroking himself. I pretended not to notice. I'd once broken up a fight in the same place, under similar circumstances, when one man took offence at another's hard-on. He didn't realise the other guy's hard-on was not inspired by him. That time, I stepped in to clarify. This time, I was relieved that Andy, like me, chose to ignore the voyeur wanking in the doorway.

John had followed me from the showers to the grooming counter, still wanking as I blowdried my hair. When I emerged from the women's changing room, he came out of the men's changing room. The timing made me wonder if he was stalking me, not merely interested in me. This was annoying. Surely he could see I was with someone.

'Are you wearing stockings?' he asked, hard-on in hand.

'No,' I said. Then I thought I'd give him enough information to help him finish himself off. 'Hold-ups, no knickers. Now leave me alone.'

'Can I see the tops of your hold-ups?' he asked.

'Sure,' I said, and pulled up my skirt and showed him the place where my hold-ups ended and my skin began. 'Now you've seen enough,' I said. 'You're taking the piss.'

'C'mon,' he pleaded. 'Can I see your pussy?'

'You've already seen that,' I said. 'Look, I'm with someone, OK? Know when to stop. You've seen plenty.'

Tantric Andy came out of the men's changing room just then, and as we moved towards the door John followed, walking a few feet behind us. I was still ignoring him when, instead of another come-on, he apologised for overstepping the mark. 'I'm sorry. I hope you didn't think I was being too rude.'

'Thanks. You were,' I said.

Andy ignored him.

So here we are again, and, even though I know he is a bit of a voyeur and I had found him an irritant the last time we met, part of me just wants to fuck him. His attentiveness, coupled with his impressive hard-on, is beginning to arouse me. I'm horny.

We go upstairs to one of the relaxation rooms. The word, of course, is a misnomer. It's not a room built for relaxation. There's no mistaking when you enter what is going to happen. A gym mat covers a wooden platform base. White tiles edge the platform, more utilitarian splashback than décor, useful for cleaning up spontaneous spillage. There's a metal receptacle on one wall for tissues, used condoms and other rubbish. It serves as the only decoration in the room.

John lays some towels down, as a kind of protective layer over the platform. It covers the who-knows-what that's gone on before. Plus, it's added comfort; it would be hard to fall asleep on such an unforgiving surface unless you padded it first with towels or had not slept for a couple of days. I love the relaxation rooms for the way they marry sleaziness with functionality.

I lie on my stomach and John starts massaging my back with baby oil. Then he moves down my leg, then between my thighs. His right hand is working the inside of my leg. The other he is using to work his own body parts. I can feel his left fist bumping rhythmically against my left leg, a telltale sign. In other words, a typical Rio's massage. I've got my head down, my eyes closed, and am relaxing into the sensations. Time passes.

'Do you want to fuck me?' I ask.

Assuming the answer is yes, I raise myself on to my knees and grab a condom from my toiletry bag. He mounts me from behind, doggy style, and slips his cock inside me. This is a position almost guaranteed to get a guy off: it facilitates deep penetration; it looks hot from the man's perspective; and it gives the guy total control. Yet after a few minutes I can feel him going soft.

When a man loses his hard-on, a girl wonders if she's the problem. Is it me? Is it because he's wearing a condom and isn't used to it or doesn't like condoms? Or does he prefer watching to fucking? Based on our history, I suspect the latter.

Still, John soldiers on, focusing on the verbal, in what I assume is an effort to stay hard. Alas, it's the usual stuff. 'You're such a slut,' he growls. 'I bet you really like being fucked by guys. Lots of guys. Lots and lots of guys.'

I say nothing.

'Should I give you more of my hard cock?'

I continue to say nothing, but think, Yes, I would like more of that hard cock, preferably a little harder than it is now. We are, after all, in a private room together.

The verbal, though not of huge interest to me, seems to work for him. His hard-on returns. 'Do you like my cock? Does it feel good inside you?'

There's no pause between his questions. He's not expecting an answer. And that's fine. I've heard it before and every word is a cliché. Guys do this because they think it turns women on. But, in my case, having had lots of sex and watched far too much porn, it just sounds ridiculous. Nothing's original anymore.

Talking dirty has its time and place, but this is neither. A monologue is a distraction. The focus becomes the words and not the actions. Used sparingly and with someone I really like, it can be turn-on. I can pretend it really is all about me and forget I've heard the same stuff come out of the mouths of lots of other men who, as in John's case, perhaps didn't fancy me quite so much. His hard-on comes and goes, and I suspect he is now fucking me more for my pleasure than his own.

About forty-five minutes have passed and he still hasn't come. I'm starting to think about the web date that I'm meeting in an hour. Not a good sign. If this guy doesn't get a move on, I think, I'm going to be late. In an effort to save him embarrassment and also pleasure myself, I take over. 'Lie down. I want to suck your cock.' There's a ninety-nine per cent chance my world-class technique will do the trick, for both of us.

I remove the condom from his cock and throw it in the rubbish bin.

I straddle one leg, my clit brushing against his thigh, while my right hand is jerking him off. My tongue does circles around the head of his cock. More time passes. I'm getting bored now, although giving him head for two minutes has aroused me more than I'd been in the previous forty-five.

'Lie down with your legs closed,' John says. I lie down on my back, legs closed. He stands on the platform by my feet and begins to wank furiously over me. 'Open your legs.' I open my legs. 'No, that's too much. Just a very little.' So I close them. 'Now open ... Now close ... Touch yourself ... Just a little.'

In my head I'm preparing the vegetable curry I've earmarked for dinner the next day. And I again think about my date that evening, and of being late, and *God, would you please hurry up? And what is it with this open-and-close thing?*

'Do you want to come?' I ask again, adding, 'I have to leave soon.'

I'm not even watching him. I'm just opening and closing my legs on command, waiting for it to be over. The blowjob was fun enough, but this is just weird. It must be horrible to have such a specific fantasy, I think. I wonder how many other girls would have put up with this shit. I wonder if he knows he hit the jackpot with me, someone patient and willing to indulge him. Most girls would have gone home half an hour ago to prepare that curry.

I'm not hating it or loving it. I'm just bored. I want to wash out the conditioner that's been medicating my scalp for the past hour and put on some make-up.

John is jerking himself off manically now, the up-and-down strokes blurring into one another. This is the best moment I've spent with him: finally, we're getting somewhere. For a change, he's silent. The wanking is taking all his concentration.

There's something so pent-up and frustrated about this guy, who has to wank so furiously to come. For most men, it's a struggle not to pop in the first five minutes. I bet the only relief John ever gets is giving himself a hand-job while looking at a porn mag.

Finally he comes. Still standing over me, his spunk projectiles out and splashes all over my tits – there's a lot of it. He looks down at me and says, 'How gross!' He sounds disgusted.

His words and tone surprise me, as much for their inappropriateness as for the sheer stupidity of the comment.

'It's *your* stuff,' I say, stating the obvious. 'How is it gross?' I'm genuinely curious to know why he'd devote so much time and effort to this performance, all for an outcome that would make him uncomfortable.

'It just is,' he says. 'Look at it.' He looks away.

I reach for a towel and begin cleaning up. 'It's your spunk,' I remind him, 'and now you're telling *me* it's weird? It is what it is. And you produced it.'

'So, are you a sex addict?' he says, not responding. 'Do you do this often?'

It occurs to me again that John probably has not done this much before. It is as if he has fulfilled a fantasy, and the outcome was anticlimactic; even though he'd climaxed, somehow it was not what he'd thought it would be. And then there was the horrible reality of come. I suspect he is quite sexually inexperienced. He is surprisingly uptight for someone who had been so aggressive in the Jacuzzi.

I feel like a sex therapist, reminding him that bodily fluids exist and are natural, that there is nothing gross about them. I could just leave, but I want to help John to understand and feel good about his own behaviour, although I don't owe this to him, and I've got a date within the hour.

'So, *are* you a sex addict? *Do* you do this often?' he asks again.

'Often enough,' I say. 'I don't know if I'm a sex addict. I just like sex. Don't you?'

He is silent.

'I'm not hurting anyone, am I? Are you?'

'But do you think you're addicted to sex?'

'Is fucking two or three different guys every couple of weeks, group sex once a month and masturbating twice a day being a sex addict? I don't know,' I say. 'But it's healthier than taking drugs or getting drunk and crashing into a tree. There are worse things in life than enjoying sex, aren't there?'

'God, I haven't fucked a stranger in years,' he says. 'I don't suppose I could have your number?'

'*So* not me,' I say, and return to the changing area.

I check my mobile phone. There's a text from the web date, saying he's knackered after playing golf all day long and won't be able to play tonight. SORRRRRRY. XXX

I drive home and am in bed before midnight.

2. THE GIRL LEAST LIKELY TO

Among my girlfriends I was always labelled 'the girl least likely to'. Girl least likely to get married, because I enjoyed sleeping around too much. Girl least likely to have children, because I never expressed much interest in kids or seemed particularly maternal. Girl least likely to do anything by the rule books, because I took pride in being unconventional.

While other friends saved themselves for marriage, I scratched notches into my bedpost. One day at the university I studied at in the States, my friend Martha challenged me to name all the guys I'd fucked since losing my virginity. Going back those five busy years, I was able to write down sixty names. There were more, but I couldn't put names to the faces.

I didn't have a great track record with relationships. It wasn't that I hadn't wanted a boyfriend all those years, but the men I met back then never seemed to stick around for long. I did like sex, though, so, when one relationship ended, I'd fuck around for a while or take up with another short-term guy to ensure I'd get laid regularly. This was pre-internet. Just like today, the number of men was unlimited, but the ways to meet them were not. So I did what a lot of girls in their twenties did then: I went to bars, clubs and parties.

When it came to men, I learnt early to take advantage of what was on offer, starting the day I lost my virginity.

I was seventeen, studying at an American school in London, and on a field trip to the Old Vic. My drama class was invited backstage to meet the cast and crew after seeing Derek Jacobi in *Hamlet*. We were introduced to Jacobi and the other players, plus a few stagehands.

'And this is Michael,' said our guide, pointing to a dramatic-looking man wearing black leather trousers and a velvet cumberbund over a flouncy white blouse. He was the lighting technician and, I thought, very glam: about ten years my senior, with sandy-blond hair like Bowie, just shy of six feet tall and quite skinny. And cute. Once I caught his eye, I stopped paying attention to Jacobi and the other stagehands. I chatted with Michael about his job, although I wasn't interested in his job.

As my classmates continued the tour, Michael quietly invited my girlfriend Laurie and me upstairs to the wig room to get stoned. We felt honoured. Then, as we were leaving, he invited us to meet him a couple of nights later at the pub next to the theatre. The opportunity to hang out with real theatre people was about as good as it got for starstruck teenage drama groupies like the two of us. And, for me, there was the promise of more on offer.

Laurie and I showed up, as arranged, and found Michael and another guy sitting at a small round table in the corner. It was a typical old-fashioned London pub – smoky, with dark-wood panelling and tobacco-stained walls, and reeking of fags and booze. We all got a little drunk, and, when Michael suggested we go back to his flat, Laurie and I readily agreed. I was excited. At last, my big night had come.

The previous year most of my girlfriends had begun talking about sex. They bragged about having lost their virginity and about sexual exploits with boys at school. They made it sound a lot more fun than shopping. There was so much emphasis on losing your virginity, I felt constrained by mine, as if not having done so set me apart as a bit of a loser. I just wanted to get rid of it.

Michael had a basement squat in a crumbling Georgian building facing Regent's Park. Inside, all the walls were painted black. We sat on the floor on Indian cushions and snogged and smoked hash. I got very stoned and found myself kissing Michael passionately. His hand reached under my top to feel my breasts, and I felt my knickers getting damp. Laurie didn't fancy Michael's friend, a long-haired hippy with spots. But I was thinking about Michael and about having sex and hoping he wouldn't notice I was still a virgin and hoping there wouldn't be any blood.

He led me to a tiny room with a large unmade double bed. I don't remember anything else about his bedroom. In my head, all I see is Michael, me and the bed. He unzipped my Brutus jeans, then pulled them down to my ankles. I unbuttoned my cheesecloth top, feeling a little scared but more excited, the adrenalin coursing through my body.

If there was any foreplay, it was minimal. I remember being kissed deeply, but I don't recall whether Michael went down on me or if I sucked his cock – that, too, would have been a first for me. What I do remember is the penetration. Michael got on top of me and thrust his cock in, hard. It hurt.

Soon it wasn't unpleasurable. He must have fucked me for an hour but I didn't come – that wouldn't happen for a year, until I went up to Cornell to visit an old school crush named Tony, who, in a memorable night for both of us, fucked me in his dorm room and gave me my first orgasm while losing his virginity. But, the night I lost mine, I was so excited, coming didn't matter. It felt good to be filled up. And to be free of my virginity.

I was sore the next day but felt great as well. I wallowed in the same relief that had followed my Bat Mitzvah a few years earlier. At thirteen, I had to study Hebrew and the Torah passage in preparation for the big day when I'd take command of the Torah. There was so much studying, so much anticipation, and then the Bat Mitzvah came and went, and I just thought, Thank God that's over. Now I can go back to hanging out with my friends.

Michael turned out to be a two-night stand, the second being a five-minute fuck in his front room while watching a BBC documentary about rabbits. He never called again. I was totally devastated. But there were other boys in whose arms I found consolation, a string of grope sessions with school classmates after one too many rum-and-cokes. They were followed in my early twenties by guys who'd ring in the middle of the night when they were drunk and horny.

A year later, at eighteen, I was wandering around Regent's Park one day, half-hoping I might run into him. I walked down his street and tried to recall the exact place where it all had happened. I couldn't remember. All the flats looked the same.

By the time I was twenty-nine and about to get married, I could have added another forty names to the list of men I'd fucked.

I called my friend Martha one day and asked what had happened to that list we'd drawn up back at university. 'I hope you didn't keep it to blackmail me, because I've met a guy. His name is David.'

Martha said we'd probably tossed the evidence, and was now very sad we'd done so. 'I should have held on to it,' she said. 'You'd have paid a lot for those historical documents, I bet.'

I assured her David knew that I had a history with men, but I didn't tell her that, like me, he just didn't know the number.

I met David at a party hosted by the actor-musician Richard Strange. It was Richard's annual Burns Night dinner and I

went with my girlfriends Adair, a journalist who had inter-
viewed Richard for a music magazine, and Lola, a costume
designer who lived next door to Richard's girlfriend. I was
working in video production then, back in London after
finishing university in the States, so felt it was my rightful scene
and came as a tagalong.

Most of the other revellers were musicians, artists or
journalists. At that time, Brixton and Herne Hill were
exploding with artistic energy, and Richard Strange was the
epitome of their cool.

We were hugely impressed to see the writer Kathy Acker
walking out as we walked in. Inside, we discovered there was
an A-list group and a B-list group. The A list included a couple
of well-known writers and actors and they got the haggis. The
B list was so large it seemed Richard had invited pretty much
everyone else he knew, however vaguely. B-listers like us
weren't invited for the dinner but came along afterwards for
leftovers and drinks.

Music from Richard's band, Cabaret Futura, was blaring on
the speakers. I was standing against a wall holding a glass of
cheap plonk when I saw a spectacularly handsome man
standing on the opposite side of the room, alone, with a beer
in his hand. He was wearing a long-sleeved cream-coloured
shirt with a busy pattern of swirling circles, straight-leg jeans
and lace-up ankle-length Doc Martens. His hair was black and
spiked on top. He was the best-looking guy I'd ever seen. And
Lola was speaking to him.

I walked over to manoeuvre an introduction.

'This is my friend Suzanne,' she said. 'Suzanne, David.' Then
she graciously walked away, leaving me to shake with nerves.

I was wearing a vintage black dress with a high neckline. I
felt good, but I didn't feel hot. This guy is so out of my league,
I thought. Yet he seemed genuinely interested in me and in no
rush to leave.

David later said it was because of my breasts. 'They were
tumbling out of your dress!' he would say, despite my protests.

'They were clearly visible, practically popping out of that low-cut dress you had on, that white thing.' Prophetically, from the start, even basic info was in conflict. Our shared memories didn't match.

We seemed to have a lot in common. We both were from the States – he grew up outside of Detroit; I was from New York. We both were in the media – I was working for a production company developing a series for Channel 4; he was managing an indie band. We both had eclectic taste in music, liked travelling and loved London.

We talked for a couple of hours, until Lola interrupted us. 'We're going now,' she said. 'I've called a minicab.'

I was staying at her place that night, so told David I had to leave, hoping he'd ask for my phone number. He did.

I looked into David's eyes and said, 'Don't you want to kiss me?' Then I stuck my tongue down his throat before he had a chance to answer. It had to be a memorable kiss, not a generic peck on the cheek.

I got the sense that was not what he was expecting. He pulled away slightly at first, then relaxed into me, and we played tongue-tag for a couple of minutes. When I heard Adair's voice telling me the minicab had arrived, I pulled away. 'Bye.'

'I'll call you,' he said.

I hoped he would, but resisted the desire to look back as I walked out the door.

David rang me up a few days later and invited me to a Glenn Branca concert at the Royal Festival Hall. It was an original choice, I thought. Most first dates consist of a quiet dinner in a romantic restaurant, not a thousand decibels of electric guitars, all nine instruments playing simultaneously. It was an intriguing start to our relationship.

We continued seeing each other, if not each other's body, over the next six weeks. We got together every few days and took it slowly. I'd cook dinner, or we'd hang out at my flat watching television. We went to movies, drove up to

Cambridge to wander around the colleges, hung out on Brighton beach – we did everything but have sex.

It was like an old-fashioned courtship. I'd never met anyone who hadn't wanted to fuck me on the first or second date. Unlike my school grope partners and the three a.m. fuck-buddies who followed them, David treated me with respect. I thought it weird that after several dates he still hadn't made a move on me, but he made up for the lack of physical affection by being amusing and sending me little postcards every few days that went straight to my heart – 'Roses are red, violets are blue, I'm bringing red wine on Friday, yahoo!' And so good to look at. He seemed to really like me and, from what he had told me about his past, he wasn't exactly a player. He'd had just five girlfriends, each of whom had lasted at least a year. It was actually refreshing to meet someone who didn't fuck around.

Still, three weeks into our relationship, I began to wonder if he was gay. Three weeks after that, I decided to find out. After drinking a bottle of wine, alone, I made a pass at him. We were on the floor, watching the telly. Enough of this, I thought. I got on top of David, ripped off his shirt and unzipped his jeans.

He was not gay – far from it. My boyfriend had a hot body and we had a very pleasant night together. We fucked for an hour or so. It was fairly straightforward stuff, a couple of positions, but, for a change, sex was intimate. And, even though I'd slept with lots of boys, I still didn't know much about sex. I came easily and I thought that was what it was all about.

Six months later David moved in with me. We tossed my futon out on the street and invested in a new king-sized Vi-Spring Herald Supreme mattress, figuring, for the price, it would last us a lifetime.

The sex was fine during our first six months together but, as on the first night we slept together, I was always the one making the first move, and after a while being the initiator ceased to be fun. And, because the positions were always the same, sex became boring. I wasn't really bothered. I was just happy to have found someone who wanted to settle down. I shrugged off the lack of sexual fireworks, figuring I'd had enough sex in school, college and all through my twenties to last a lifetime.

Shortly after David moved in, we booked a last-minute package to a small Greek island called Spetses. Neither of us had much money then, but we shared the desire to escape the sticky summer heat of London. Another thing we had in common was that neither of us had ever heard of Spetses before – for good reason, as we later discovered. It didn't matter where we went. I secretly hoped a romantic holiday would break the routine and rekindle our sex life.

The trip was a disaster from the start. Indeed, just leaving the UK was a challenge. Our afternoon flight out of Gatwick was delayed and, after waiting three hours, David announced he wanted to cancel the trip and go home. 'This is ridiculous,' he said, eyeing the harried rep at the gate. 'This is unprofessional. I'm going up there to demand a refund – a full refund.'

'Hold on,' I said, and looked at our travel ticket. The fine print promised refunds, but only on flights delayed more than fifteen hours. 'Twelve hours to go, darling. Sorry.'

After we arrived at our seaside hotel, the bed collapsed as David sat on it. The next morning, the toilet broke. The beaches, which had looked so magnificent in the brochures, did not make up for these little irritations, as they were cluttered with empty water bottles, beer cans and tubes of suntan lotion, discarded, we decided, by previous waves of disillusioned tourists, most of them English. We had come to experience Greek life and instead found an English resort on the Mediterranean. There were British pubs, British accents and British people everywhere we went. Other couples might have laughed it off and stayed in their hotel rooms to fuck away their disappointment. But the stress of the holiday failed as an aphrodisiac, and by the end of the trip we were barely speaking.

David exploded on the last day, while arguing with me over directions. His rage was so inappropriate it spooked me and made me wonder if a relationship with him was worth the stress. Feeling I had few other options, I stuck it out.

I often wonder how different my life would be had I walked away back then. I was twenty-eight and still young enough to find another life partner, maybe even one who would also be a sex partner. But there were no other guys in the queue. So I signed on to the usual routine: got married, had a couple of kids, gained weight.

Dressing one morning a few years into our marriage, I looked in the mirror and thought, I've become everything I said I'd never be. I was the frumpy, overweight, undersexed mother I'd seen all my life in the grocery stores. I was two stone over my ideal weight and wore baggy Marks & Spencer clothes to hide my bulging stomach. When I'd met David, I was vibrant – a pushy New York Jewish broad turned London punkette. I'd never hesitated to flirt with the best-looking guy at a party or stick my tongue down his throat. At university, in the States, I was the chick from London who wore fashions six months ahead of others' radar, whose purple hair and ripped fishnet stockings and mini-kilts caused more than one student to cross the street when they saw me coming. Now, a generic mother and an ignored wife, I was living my life to ensure everyone else's happiness and had forgotten to nurture my own.

Had I been getting laid more often, this might have been tolerable. But my unfulfilling sex life was one thing I knew would never change. Six years into our marriage, even the monthly couplings came to an end. It happened the night I orgasmed so loudly David laughed at me. He was on the bottom, as usual, and was about to come when my own orgasm derailed him. It was quite high volume, admittedly. I felt him go soft beneath me. He was looking up at me, laughing. It was a nervous laugh, as if I had embarrassed him after committing a faux pas. Instantly it struck me that my husband saw no beauty in giving me an orgasm and, worse, took no joy in my pleasure.

It was hardly the first time he'd given me an orgasm. In fact, I always came during sex – one lesson I learnt early on was to get as much pleasure from my partners as they got from me. Maybe that night I was more vocal than usual, but David laughed at me, not with me, and his laughter made me uncomfortable. That night I felt a wall come down on my emotions. I knew I would never fuck my husband again. How could I relax during sex? How could I feel desire for someone who laughed at me when I came? Suddenly, I felt nothing for the man with whom I shared my bed. I turned over and went to sleep.

Gradually I lost all desire. More than once I thought to myself, Even if Richard Gere pulled down his trousers and flashed a massive hard-on, I'd say, 'Not tonight, Richard.' The uncommon girl had the most common inventory of problems, the kind dissected in all the women's magazines. And how salt-in-the-wound pathetic that the good-time, go-to girl was now living like a nun.

I have an iffy memory for dates. I can remember my family's birthdays and the date I got married, of course. I can never remember my parents' wedding anniversary or those of my brothers, though, or the date I got divorced or even the month I graduated university. But 14 May 2000 stands out as if I'd memorised it as a kid, along with 4 July 1776 and 25 December. Nothing particularly novel happened that day: I went to work, as usual; I came home, gave the kids their dinner and put them to bed, as usual. But later that night everything changed for me.

The evening started with cocktails at Groucho's, a members-only club in the West End popular with pop stars and writers and the hipsters who'd beat its two-year waiting list. I'd never been there before and went with a client, a dance producer named Aidan who was a member of the club; my girlfriend

Janie, a journalist; and Aidan's friend, a man he introduced as Nigel. Groucho's had a large dimly lit room filled with comfortable sofas and plump armchairs, with walls lined with 19th-century etchings from the *Illustrated London News* and a dark walnut bar along one side. And – I was happy to see – famous people, in the flesh. It was exciting to be somewhere so glamorous, and so liberating to be out of the house and in the world of adults. Since becoming a mother, I'd hardly gone anywhere except to the office and the babycare aisle at Sainsbury's.

That night Robbie Williams was hanging out at a nearby table and Keith Allen was at the piano serenading friends, who were laughing loudly at his made-up lyrics to familiar tunes. Janie wanted to run up to Robbie Williams and tell him he was a sex bomb. I told her, if she did, I'd never speak to her again; I hadn't been out for a million years, but I still knew what was uncool. It was a Friday night and Aidan, Janie and I were celebrating the end of a project with dinner in the club's restaurant; Nigel was there for the ride. I'd been promoting a well-known dancer whom Aidan had produced and Janie had written about for a national newspaper. The reviews weren't so great, but the shows had sold out, so everyone was happy and in good spirits.

I got a little drunk and was feeling loose and horny. I looked over at Aidan's friend and said, 'So, what do you do, Nigel?'

'I'm resting at the moment.'

'Resting?'

'Not working. I decided to take a rest for a while.'

He didn't elaborate and didn't seem particularly interested in carrying on the conversation either, so I waited until he went to the toilet before getting the goods.

'How can a man who doesn't look forty afford to "rest" for a living, Aidan?'

Aidan told me Nigel had once managed a famous band and, when things turned sour, sued them in a dispute over management fees and walked away with £10 million.

Suddenly, the heat turned up on Nigel. When I'd met my husband, he was on the dole. Although he was now a successful marketing executive, he didn't have £10 million in the bank. I'd never been out with a rich man in my life.

'He did all right,' Aidan continued. 'Then he skipped the country to avoid paying tax – left his wife and kids for a year and went travelling. He said one day he looked up at the departures board and realised there was no place else he wanted to see. So he got on a plane and came home.'

'And now he's at Groucho's, the shit,' I said.

Although he barely said a word, I found Nigel more and more intriguing with each glass of Meursault I drank over dinner. I hated myself for wondering if it was only because he was the richest man I'd ever met. I'd never even considered having an affair since meeting David, but, as I looked at Nigel across the table, I began imagining all the things we could do together with so much cash: have a shopping spree at Harvey Nichols, spend a weekend in Paris at the George V, buy a pied-à-terre in New York.

So illusive, so unwilling to give away anything about himself, Nigel sparked fantasies he might be hiding more than just a £10-million stash. Like a big cock. He paid no more attention to me than to anyone else at the table. But that didn't stop me from wondering if behind that silent exterior lay someone who'd make me scream in bed. It was the first time in years I'd thought about another man or found another man desirable. That night, Nigel, or my fantasy of Nigel, made me feel something I had not felt in nearly a decade: arousal.

When I got home, it was three a.m. But, instead of going to bed, I turned on the computer.

I typed 'free porn' into the MSN search engine, hoping a preview clip on some dodgy Triple-X website would pop up – pictures of big black cocks, gang bangs, deep-throat blowjobs or, my personal favourite, glory holes. After five minutes of visuals, my fingers stroking my clit, I'd be off to bed and able to sleep. The computer had replaced my sex life ever since I'd stopped fucking my husband three years earlier; self-induced orgasms had become my sleeping pill.

Secretly, in the middle of the night, I used to lie in bed masturbating, silently and slowly replaying fantasy scenes I'd seen on the web. I'd always found porn kind of sexy – equal parts sleazy and sexy, forbidden and mundane. When sex between David and I began to wane, I'd told him that if he wanted to see me really turned on, all he had to do was find some hardcore pornography.

'That's really sick,' he said, and that was the end of that option.

Microsoft, the bland corporate entity that it is, isn't much more adventurous. On the night of 14 May, when I typed the words 'free porn', what came up at the top of the list was a stylish erotic online magazine called Nerve. It wasn't what I was looking for: no glory holes, no big black cocks – indeed, no porn. It was just poetry and other people's fictional stories, plus a few arty black-and-white photographs, mainly of attractive women with nice boobs – lovely to look at, but not my thing at all, at least not since the age of twenty-two, when I'd finished groping my way through a bi phase.

I trawled the site, hoping to find at least one photo of a cute guy with a hard-on. Instead I found a personals section. I hadn't known such a thing existed online and decided to have a look, curious to see what kind of people posted themselves on the web.

The personals were laid out like a questionnaire. Each person had to answer the same ten questions. 'What's the sexiest scene in the movies?' was one. 'Name some music that really turns you on' was another. The questions were more insipid than erotic, but they got me thinking it might be fun to have a pen pal, just like I'd had when I was ten years old. So I posted a personal. I typed 'Friendship L'Amour' in the heading, oblivious in my late-night stupor to the English–French disconnect – friendship *and* love? – and counting on the sexless word 'friendship' to keep away the pervs. Before uploading my personal I had to enter a postcode. There were options only for people living in the States, however, so I entered random numbers with no idea where they would place me on the map. Location was irrelevant; I was only looking for a pen pal, not to meet someone, and the fact that all the men on Nerve lived in the US seemed a bonus. It made everything feel safe and free of complications.

Aside from my husband, who worked long hours and rarely spoke about anything outside of work, I had no close male friends. I hadn't had a proper two-way conversation with a man since getting married nine years earlier. I naïvely thought there might be a man out there in a similar situation who also wanted an email buddy. I uploaded my personal, forgot about big black cocks and glory holes, and went to sleep.

3. MY LIBERATOR

The day after I posted my personal on Nerve, I had to do some errands and couldn't wait to get home so I could check my inbox. There were five messages. It was gratifying knowing even one person wanted to write to me, particularly as I'd stressed friendship, not a relationship. I was as excited as I'd been at the age of ten, when I'd received my first newsletter after joining the Jackson 5 Fan Club.

One guy said he was a fifty-seven-year-old biker who ran a Harley shop in Los Angeles. Another claimed to be an investment banker in Chicago. A third told me he was a graphic designer from Seattle. A fourth was a New York City lawyer. I never did find out what the fifth guy did; he just sent a picture of his big cock – something I wished I'd seen the night before – and asked what I was into. I looked at the cock shot for a minute, then hit Delete.

Soon enough, as my pen pals realised I'd truly joined Nerve to chat, not have cybersex, the four dropped down to one. His name was Frank, the lawyer. He had an office in Times Square and a wife he'd been married to for twenty years. Like me, he had two kids about the age of my own and wasn't looking for a relationship.

We had many things in common. Frank lived in a neighbourhood not far from where my grandmother had lived – in Queens, a borough across the East River from Manhattan full of anonymous high-rise apartment blocks. Frank's wife had been brought up in a small blue-collar town on Long Island just five miles from where I lived until moving to England at thirteen. At one point, our fathers even worked for the same company.

I imagined a pudgy middle-aged man, with thinning grey hair. I pictured him sitting in a sack suit, in a large office, behind a large walnut desk, the chaos of Times Square erupting just outside his window. Like me, Frank had not posted a photo on his profile, and I didn't care. I wasn't planning on meeting him, so it didn't matter what he looked like. We were just two people getting to know one another through words.

Frank seemed to want to know everything about me and was interested in hearing what I had to say. Day after day I would come home from work and go straight to the computer to check my inbox. I found myself looking forward to going home. My husband had never been particularly curious about my background, so I suppose it was natural I enjoyed sharing my life story with someone who was genuinely interested.

I told Frank about a dream I had one night that puzzled me. Just when I thought my sexual feelings had ceased to exist, I dreamt about working as a bank teller in an old-fashioned bank where everyone sat behind protective glass. In the dream, a cute younger man in his early twenties worked next to me. We were attracted to each other but were separated by the glass. We couldn't kiss in the bank, so we ran outside and found ourselves in a field. We kissed passionately for a very long time. I remember being on the verge of waking and not wanting the dream to end, but then waking and thinking how real the dream had felt. I was convinced my mouth and tongue had moved while I slept.

The dream puzzled me because it reminded me of similar kissing dreams I experienced first as a teenager and that never really went away. I told Frank I attributed it to a lifelong desire to relive the nourishing promise of a passionate first kiss with an attractive stranger. After I stopped sleeping with my husband, I told Frank, I'd think about those old dreams and wonder if I would ever feel such passion again.

'I really like being your pen pal,' he wrote one day. 'I wonder what you look like, smell like, sound like.'

I wondered what he looked like and smelt like and sounded like, too. But, because I still did not know what he looked like, I was free to use my imagination. I did not picture the image of a full-arm tattoo, however – the work-in-progress Frank admitted to in an email one day. 'Hurt like a bitch,' he admitted. 'But I'm not averse to a little pain.'

His comment barely registered, but the idea of a full-arm tattoo did. I'm not keen on tattoos, but the way Frank described his quest – seeking out an internationally recognised tattoo artist, Vyvyn Lazonga; planning the design, a dragon wrapped around his arm; researching the origins and mythology of the art – impressed me. Certainly it was not the standard girlfriend's-name-in-a-heart motif. My perception of Frank changed dramatically. Now I really wanted to know what he looked like.

'I think of you often. You're becoming a narcotic to me,' he wrote a month into our correspondence. 'But it's frustrating that I only know parts of you.'

I felt the same way.

The next day in my inbox was a brief note from Frank. 'Here's a picture. I hope you can open it.'

My heart quickened as I double-clicked on the attachment. Until that moment I had not understood the power of the internet, the way it creates a false intimacy. Suddenly there was a real person at the other end of the email.

I watched his picture download little by little on my slow dial-up connection. The image staring back at me showed a slim attractive man with short dark hair, thin lips and an intense gaze. He had sad eyes, but, knowing Frank's wasn't the happiest marriage, I wondered if I were reading too much into the visuals. He was not as handsome as my husband, but I saw similarities in their faces and bodies. Both had a runner's physique, dark hair, high cheekbones. Same type, but a different man altogether. Now I really was hooked. But first I needed to know what my fantasy man sounded like.

A man's voice has always been a powerful aphrodisiac for me. Once, while at university, I broke up with the best-looking guy on campus simply because I couldn't stand listening to the sound of his voice. Ironically, we met in a voice-and-diction class – we were both communications majors – when he sat next to me on the first day. What a hunk! I thought – until he turned to me before class began and asked in a whiny high-pitched voice made worse by a thick Brooklyn accent, 'Do you think they can help me change my voice?'

'Well, they don't work miracles,' I replied dryly.

He forgave my lack of diplomacy. We had sex in my dorm room that afternoon after class. I had been wearing a pair of leopard-print Spandex spray-on pants, a ripped purple T-shirt and pink pointy 1960s flats. He had on an Italian-cut suit, tassled loafers and a pale-blue button-down Brooks Brothers shirt. We were the style king and queen of the class, albeit on opposite ends of the spectrum, and recognised in each other our mutual vanity. I found out he not only looked good, he also had a pretty big cock and knew what to do with it. Unfortunately, I never got over the voice and cut things off within three months. Lesson learnt: if they keep their mouths shut and their pants down, they're fine. Since then, I've made a point of never dating a man whose voice I don't like.

'I want to hear your voice,' I wrote to Frank. 'Send me your number. Please.'

'Not a good idea, Suzanne. We're both married. Let's keep things the way they are.'

I continued to ask for his number and, after eight weeks of emailing each other, Frank finally relented. The daily two-page emails turned into one- or two-hour phone calls. I'd come home from work, start to prepare dinner and ring Frank. With the time difference, it would be his lunch hour.

He had a strong New York accent, more Jimmy Stewart nasal than Al Pacino grunt. I had had a different voice in mind – deeper, smoother, more seductive, like an American DJ or the voiceovers for American movie trailers. Still, it worked for me and, two weeks after our first phone call, Frank gave me his home number. I could call any time over the next month, he said, because his wife and kids would be in Texas visiting her parents.

'Wow, a whole month on your own,' I said. 'Want company?'

'Are you serious?'

I assured him I was, and in my head began concocting a scheme to get out of town. Then I did something I had not done in ten years: I lied to David. I told him I had to go to New York to visit Martha, who had just had a baby. The fact that I had not spoken to my old college friend in three years didn't strike him as unusual, nor did my desire to see Martha's new baby, even though several friends in London had popped out offspring in recent years that somehow I'd never managed to see. Whether a testament to his trust in me or proof of how little he really understood me, David bought my lie. And why wouldn't he? I had never lied before, except to defend the occasional hideous haircut or to shave a few pounds off the price of some Sergio Rossi shoes I'd bought.

Once I booked the flight, I was like a cat in heat. I'd hang up after a conversation with Frank and find my knickers dripping wet. I began to go back to the office after putting the kids to bed, having told David I had work to do – more lies tarnishing my wifely record – and ring Frank at his office and have phone sex. Frank would lock his office door and we'd masturbate together, three thousand miles apart.

As the departure date grew closer, I ached with desire, truly ached – my pussy throbbed. It was physically painful. I thought only of being filled by him.

I trimmed my hair from a mid-shoulder cut to a short, layered bob. I went to Selfridges and Agent Provocateur and Fuk.com and picked up tasty outfits, one size too small as an incentive. And I went on a starvation diet, eating just two meals a day, skipping the highest calories of dinnertime. My nutrition was mental, anyway – I lived on sexual fantasies. In the evening I'd jump on my treadmill and run for forty-five minutes, to ensure my elevated metabolism burnt extra calories while I slept. I wanted to lose a stone before I got to New York in four weeks. I wanted Frank to think I was hot and want to fuck me as soon as he saw me.

Almost three months to the day we began our correspondence, and hundreds of calls and emails later, I was hailing a taxi at Kennedy Airport, heading for the W Hotel in Times Square. It was central, and on the Net it looked hip and romantic. The room was about as big as the king-sized bed in it, with perhaps two feet free on either side. That was fine with me. I took a shower, washed my hair, lotioned and potioned all over, then put on my new pink Frank T-shirt vest, a denim skirt and blue sandals.

'What kind of clothes turn you on?' Frank had asked before I left London to meet him for the first time. Most men look good in black, so I specified black jeans, a black T-shirt and cowboy boots – a *Midnight Cowboy* fantasy. It was a fail-safe uniform for a tall guy with a slim body, plus it reminded me of so many guys I'd seen in the clubs when I was in my twenties. It seemed fitting, somehow, in this newly sexual life of mine, to dress this man like the ones I'd undressed in my earlier sexual days. Even though I hoped he'd be taking off his clothes as soon as he saw me, I didn't want to risk Frank showing up in naff clothes, such as a checked shirt or cheap jeans or his work suit. I had already constructed the fantasy in my head of what would happen, and I wanted to make sure that, near as damn it, it would turn out that way.

At six p.m., two hours after my arrival, I heard a knock. I opened the door to a man wearing black jeans, a black T-shirt and cowboy boots. Frank did not look like his photo or the picture that had developed in my mind. He was not in the same league as my husband, but then not many men are. He had heavy eyelids and skin so pale it suggested a person who spent far too long in front of a PC. He was actually somewhat geeky looking, but then Frank *was* a geek; he'd been a maths major in college and one of his hobbies was playing computer chess, a fact I suddenly remembered as I stared at the man at the door. There was a brief moment when I said to myself, 'You can say no.' But then I thought, You've come three thousand miles to see this guy, Suzanne – don't turn him away.

He smiled at me awkwardly and said, 'Hello, Suzanne.'

For once in your life, I thought, look beyond the surface.

Frank came into the room and we hugged awkwardly. Then I moved my lips towards his. Our tongues met. His breath was warm, his mouth soft and wet. He pulled back, but I leant into him. I wanted a second taste. I had never had a kiss like that before, one that made me feel lightheaded. I actually felt dizzy. Pheromones? Endorphins? It was a chemical reaction, pure animal attraction.

Instinctively, we both moved to the bed and continued kissing. Frank slipped his hand underneath my skirt and felt between my legs, where it was already moist. We didn't speak at all.

I pulled my top over my head.

'Stop. Slow down,' said Frank. 'Let's take it slow. I want to savour every moment.'

Slowly he removed the left strap off my shoulder, then the right, until just my breasts were holding up my bra. His hands lingered on my arm for a moment before reaching behind to undo the clasp. Every gesture, every moment had voyeuristic implications for Frank. He was his own cameraman, as if recording the actions in his head for playback at a later date.

My bra fell away from my body and on to the floor and he looked at my breasts. 'You are so beautiful,' he said.

I hadn't heard a compliment from a man for years. Then, not ten minutes after meeting me, Frank did something my husband had never done in the ten years we'd been together. He went down on me.

He lifted up my denim skirt, then paused before pulling down my silk knickers, taking in the sight intently. As Frank began licking my pussy, I thought about blood. My period had come that day and I was worried he might be put off by it. As every woman knows, it isn't every man's cup of tea; it makes some men uncomfortable, is messy and can be a turn-off.

'I'm sorry. I've got my period,' I said, stating the obvious.

'Doesn't bother me,' he said from below. He stayed down there for twenty minutes, until I reminded him we had a dinner reservation at Lotus.

We looked at each other, half-embarrassed, half-excited. Frank had blood on his face and hands. The white sheets were spotted with red handprints. We had been together for half an hour and already the room looked like a crime scene.

'Your pussy tastes delicious,' said Frank. 'We'll resume this later.'

Here was a man who lived to eat pussy, I happily realised. It was his thing. He preferred it to all other forms of sex, he said as we talked in the shower before leaving for dinner. Lucky me. He found oral sex relaxing, meditative, an almost spiritual act, he said. After a decade of oral abstinence, I was plenty ready for his religion.

Over dinner, Frank confessed his own fears about our meeting. 'My anxiety grew with each step,' he explained. 'Across town, to the hotel, through the lobby, up the elevator, down the corridor. Each step, Suzanne.' He said he had stood outside my door before knocking, listening to the sounds on the other side.

Lotus was half-empty – it was still early evening – so our waiter left us alone. Frank's hand travelled up my leg and fingered the edge of my knickers. We looked intensely into each other's eyes, like two teenagers on their first date. I felt embarrassed but also excited by the attention. As we sat in the restaurant, barely able to keep our hands off each other, I stroked his hard cock through his trousers and he fingered my pussy under my dress. 'If this room were empty, these fingers would make you come right here, Suzanne.'

I'd never met an exhibitionist before. Frank was French kissing me between courses, and, when he wasn't fingering me, he was nibbling on my ear and threatening to pull off my knickers. I could see from the smile on his face he was getting off on the glances we were attracting from the other diners. We skipped dessert and went back to the W for a three-hour pudding.

I spent the next three days on my back, punctuated by brief rest periods for eating and a little sleeping. After three years of total celibacy, I was insatiable. We fucked for breakfast, then wandered the streets of New York before coming back to our room for an afternoon round. Frank would work for a few hours while I caught up on my sleep. Then we fucked again before dinner. When we weren't fucking, we were kissing, touching, groping each other. I couldn't believe my luck, and Frank seemed to feel the same. He was constantly hard and I was constantly wet. I thought we were a perfect match.

Yet nothing is ever truly perfect. Frank wouldn't come, or couldn't, even though, only halfway through the weekend, he had given me five orgasms. I began to wonder if something was wrong, but said nothing at first. On our last day, while lying in bed after yet another marathon session, I said, 'You haven't come all weekend. Don't you want to?'

He didn't seem that bothered by it. 'I don't have to come. I just love seeing you come.'

I'd never heard of a man who didn't want or need to come. I felt like I'd failed in some way. 'Well, if you wanted to come, what would I need to do?'

'I need you to tell me you hate me,' he said.

'But I don't hate you,' I said, confused. 'That would be lying.'

'Tell me you hate me,' he repeated. 'I need you to tell me you hate me.'

'I don't think I can do that, Frank.'

I did not understand what he was asking me to do, or why. I had flown three thousand miles to meet someone with whom I had become more intimate than I was with my own husband. How could he think I could tell him such a thing? Why would he have wanted to meet me so badly, and been so loving towards me, if he wanted me to hate him?

'Tell me you hate me,' he pleaded.

This was not my idea of a proper relationship, of love, of sex even – accommodating someone who wanted to be abused. I wanted to make him come, but not this way.

Frank could see I was uncomfortable and, seeking to avoid further discomfort, he said, 'Don't worry. I won't ask you again.' He didn't sound disappointed, just defeated.

We had sex three more times that weekend. I always came; he never did.

'You know,' I told him as I was leaving, 'I may never see you again.' It had taken a huge lie to bring us together this one time, and I didn't know if I wanted to do it again, especially for a masochist.

When I returned to London, there was an email from Frank. 'Sorry about that psychosexual favour I asked you,' he wrote. 'I'm sorry it made you uncomfortable. I always have to make things hard. But that's the way it's always been for me.' He said that in only two days I had clued into an aspect of him that had taken his wife fifteen years to work out: he wasn't the thoroughbred of any woman's dreams.

Perhaps Frank wasn't quite a dream man after all, but he did make me feel attractive and desired and special. The more I thought about him and the longer we continued our long-distance relationship, the more determined I became to return to New York and find a way to make him come.

I resolved to stay married, keep my family life and fly to New York every three months, each time concocting a new lie to justify my exit. On my second visit I learnt how to make Frank come.

We were having sex – Frank on top, my legs wrapped around his back. 'Tell me about the men you've fucked,' he said. 'What were they like? What did they do to you? I know you've fucked loads of guys.'

It had been a decade since I'd fucked anyone besides my husband, but I'd had plenty of lovers before David. I thought back to my early twenties and told Frank about an assistant director named Tim whom I met in a West End pub.

'He used to ring me up in the middle of the night when he was drunk,' I said. 'He'd ask what I was doing, and I'd tell him I'd been asleep. "Why don't you come over and fuck me and my mate?" he'd say. I didn't like his friend, so I'd just fuck Tim and let his friend watch. Sometimes I'd suck his cock and let his friend watch that, too. There wasn't enough room on the double mattress for all of us, so I'd usually call a cab after the sex.'

Frank started to pump me harder. He arched his back and pushed into me. It felt brilliant.

'Did he have a big cock?' he asked.

'Yes. That's why I went over there.'

Frank didn't have a big cock, and it was not very thick, but feeling him get harder and seeing him get more excited as I told my stories made me wet and turned me on.

'Tell me about someone else,' he pleaded.

So I told him about a guy from university whom I used to see riding his expensive racing bike around campus, in skin-tight biking gear. I fucked him because he looked arrogant and I thought it would be satisfying to demolish his ego. 'One day

I left a note on his bike saying I'd seen him around and wanted to fuck him. I wrote down my dorm-room number and said I'd be in at seven that night. And, like an obedient puppy, he showed up, on the dot. I sat on his cock until I came, then pulled him out and jerked him off. After he came, I said, "OK, you have to go now. I'm really busy."'

'You're such a slut,' Frank said, pumping harder. 'I knew you were a slut. You're just using me.'

My stories had the desired effect. I may not have been able to say 'I hate you', but there were other things I could do to make him feel used, like a human dildo. After two more stories about guys I'd fucked, he climaxed.

It wasn't easy at first. It didn't come naturally to share my sexual history while making love. It felt sordid and wrong, like I was a cheap hooker there to get a trick off before moving on to the next guy. But, if that was what would make Frank come, then that was what I wanted to do.

By the end of my second visit, I'd grown used to it, and it even began to turn me on to see the effect my words had on him. I may have fucked a hundred men before I got married, at twenty-nine, but it was now ten years on and the details of those early encounters were sketchy. So soon I was making up stories about guys with enormous cocks who made me suck them off until I was gagging, who fucked me hard, who shot their spunk all over my body.

When we weren't in bed, Frank liked to show me off. He acted like a man who'd won first prize at the state fair and wanted to display his trophy. He kissed me on the street, touched my breasts in stores, fingered me under the table at restaurants. One hot afternoon Frank and I were walking around Greenwich Village. I was wearing a thin white Fruit of the Loom men's vest with a pair of cut-off jeans slashed to the top of my thighs. We stopped to make out on the steps of a townhouse. I felt Frank's hands move beneath my vest and begin removing my bra. He reached around to feel my hard nipples before unclasping the bra and sliding it off under my shirt. I reached down and felt his crotch. He was hard. 'Let's go back to the hotel,' I said. Exhibitionist, masochist, piece of work. But what a lay!

'Your shirt's pretty see-through,' Frank said, not moving from the townhouse steps. He got off on the idea that passers-by could see my nipples and his hard-on. I was relieved I was on the other side of the ocean from home, but he never seemed concerned he might run into someone he knew, someone who knew he was married.

On my third visit to New York, Frank took public display to the next level. He suggested we find a swinging club. 'It's something I've always wanted to try out,' he explained, 'but I've never met anyone who'd do it with me.'

It was not something I'd ever considered. I told him the closest I'd come to an orgy occurred back in university, at a house party in the arty seaside town of Portsmouth, New Hampshire. A guy I met – cute but off his tits on coke – suggested group sex. 'Let's see if we can round up some people,' he said. 'See you back here in a half-hour.'

I walked around the house in search of willing participants. There were no takers, it being Puritan New England, so the two of us got on with it anyway and fucked in the coat room for three hours, interrupted now and then by people asking us to move so they could retrieve their coats, which we'd been using as a mattress.

'I'd love to watch you fuck another guy,' Frank said. 'It would really turn me on – watching you suck another man's cock while I fuck you from behind.'

'Would you really like to see me fuck another guy?' I asked. 'Wouldn't you get jealous?'

'I don't know,' he said. 'If so, we could always leave.' He said he had heard of a couple of sex clubs in the city and promised to check them out on the web.

The next night he took me to a place of dubious legality and no name, the one that, at $60 per couple, was the cheapest of several options. I wore a tight, very short leopard-print PVC dress with slits up the thighs. My best girlfriend, Bernadette, gave it to me for my birthday before I left London. She and I had talked about Frank a lot. She said I needed something uber-sexy for the next time I saw my man. A pair of black six-inch stiletto shoes completed the porn-star look.

Our taxi dropped us outside a rented venue in TriBeCa that was nondescript on the outside and disappointingly nonsexual on the inside. I didn't know what to expect, but assumed I'd see beds or love swings or bondage equipment. And people. Instead, there were empty bar stools and an empty dance floor. Fifteen minutes after our arrival, a couple came in. We watched them walk through a back door and down stairs I had assumed led to the bar's basement. When a second couple arrived and did the same, we realised where the action was.

We followed them downstairs and entered what looked like a storage room, just a collection of chairs and a few old sofas and square café tables against the walls. Still no beds in sight, but the anxious-looking bouncer we passed at the bottom of the stairs made it clear we were in the right place. My sense was that he was on the lookout to make sure the club didn't get busted. It made me wonder if at any minute the police might bust in and arrest people for – what, indecent exposure? Still, that didn't dissuade us.

There were five other couples there, already well into each other. On one side of the room, a half-decent-looking white guy, about forty years old, with short dark hair, wearing an unbuttoned shirt and black trousers pulled down to his knees, was being sucked off by a naked woman with shoulder-length blonde hair. His fingers were exploring the pussy of another woman, who was seated beside him. She looked to be in her late thirties and was wearing a purple blouse and a matching skirt hitched up her thighs. Nearby a mixed-race couple was fucking on one of the sofas.

The room was quiet except for the heavy breathing and sexual sighing coming from the other side of the room. There was no music. We took a seat on a large sofa next to a man and a woman who were taking in the show. It was a turn-on watching other people having sex. Another couple was sitting a good twenty feet away, just far enough that one couldn't quite work out what they were doing. Were his fingers in her pussy or playing with her clit? How big was his cock? And what was the relationship of the dark-haired guy and his two women? Were they together?

I wanted to be part of it all but didn't know where to begin. We didn't know the rules and didn't know if it was appropriate to speak or engage with the others. 'We are virgins,' I said to Frank. 'Here, at least.'

'What a novelty,' he said. 'Let's lose our virginity, baby.'

Frank put two tables together and told me to lie down on them and dangle my legs over one side. He positioned himself in a chair, lifted my dress, and started licking my pussy. I closed my eyes, not to tune out the scene in the room but to concentrate on my own physical sensations.

Although aroused, after thirty minutes I still couldn't come. No one had approached us, which would have enlivened things, and I found the noises in the room a distraction.

'Your turn,' I said. I told Frank to sit on the sofa. I leant down in front of him, took a pillow off the sofa and put it under my knees to soften the hard floor. I unzipped his trousers, pulled out his cock and took it in my mouth. The couple nearby looked over, as though seeing us for the first time.

In retrospect, my first exposure to swinging was quite pedestrian. I played only with Frank and he only with me. We didn't swap partners. We didn't make contact with anyone else. The only difference was that we had sex in a room where there were other people, so in that sense it wasn't all that different from my failed orgy in Portsmouth, New Hampshire. Even so, it felt daring and new and liberating – and very different from my daily life in London.

About a month after I returned from my third weekend with Frank, my husband discovered my secret Nerve account. He had been mining our email system for a friend's address, and instead found an alert Nerve had sent me. 'A message is waiting for you,' said the subject header. It should have said, 'You wanted to get fucked. Well, now you *are* fucked.'

He confronted me in the kitchen when he came home from work. 'Why would you need another account?' he asked. 'What's Nerve.com?'

I could feel my stomach clench. My hands started to shake. My cover was blown. I'd always been a terrible liar, and keeping my affair secret had been incredibly difficult.

'There's a few personal matters I'm dealing with,' I said lamely. 'I didn't want to use my work email.'

'What kind of personal issues? What have you got to hide?' he asked.

I couldn't think of anything to say, so I told him the truth. 'I'm seeing someone else.'

'Really?' said David. He looked genuinely surprised. 'Who?'

I had expected shouting or anger or disappointment. Instead, he looked puzzled. He hadn't had sex with me for so long, I wondered if he found incomprehensible the idea of anyone else having sex with me. He looked almost calm.

'A guy in New York,' I explained. 'We met over the web. That's who I've been visiting on my trips there.'

'Wow. That was very conniving of you.' He sounded almost approving. He asked my lover's name and what he did for a living. I said his name was Frank, that he was a lawyer, was married, had two kids, lived in Queens.

'Wow.'

I expected more than a wow. Still, I was relieved. I hadn't been chucked out of the house on my ass. And I no longer had to keep a secret. As for David, he seemed almost relieved himself. Maybe, like me, he preferred honesty to all else. There was a man between us, but at least no more lies. He walked out of the kitchen without saying another word.

A couple of days later, I asked my parents if they would babysit so David and I could go out for dinner. Then I burst out crying. They asked what the problem was, and I told them about Frank and admitted I'd been unhappy in my marriage. My father asked if David and I had sex any more. I told him it had been years.

'It's over,' he said. 'If you don't have sex, you don't have a relationship. It's finished.'

David and I went to a Lebanese place off the Edgware Road. It was still early and the restaurant was empty. We sat opposite each other. He seemed remarkably calm. Anyone passing our table would have thought we were an average married couple on an average night out.

'What's going on?' I asked. 'You're not pissed off. What's happening?' I ran through various scenarios. Was he relieved? Had he fallen out of love with me, as I had with him? Did he even care? I looked over and saw David squirming in his seat, a guilty expression on his face. 'You're not actually turned on, are you?'

He was looking down at his lap. 'Well,' he began. He was silent for a moment. 'I might be.'

'You're actually turned on by the thought of me with another man?'

'I might be,' he repeated. It seemed more an admission than a theory.

Now it was my turn to be shocked. I realised that after ten years I didn't really know my husband at all. The man who I thought was shy in bed was secretly turned on by the thought of me with another man. It was something I couldn't have foreseen. We'd never spoken about sex, about our desires or fantasies. We just did it. And, like so many young couples, we'd quickly settled into a pattern whereby one initiated and the other acquiesced, except it was always me who made the first move. Beyond that, I knew nothing about his sexual cosmology.

'Now that you're having sex with another man,' he continued, 'maybe you'll want to have sex with me again, too.'

I wondered about his motives. Did he really want me? Or did he think of sex as the price to keep his personal chef, laundress, errand-runner and caretaker? The one thing I was sure of was this: fucking David wasn't an option. My affair finally forced us to communicate, but it was too late for the two of us.

'It doesn't work that way, David. I can't just push a button and turn on, like a machine. I'm in love with this man. That's why I have sex with him. I can't fuck you. I'm sorry.'

He was silent for a moment. 'So what do you want to do?' he asked.

'I want a divorce.'

Again, he didn't look stunned or upset. He just said, 'OK. If that's what you want.' And then my husband became a businessman again. 'But I don't want to have to do loads of paperwork. If you want a divorce, you get the lawyer, you do everything. And if you want to see this guy in the States,' he added, 'go ahead, but just don't tell the kids.'

We played out the happy-family rituals until the paperwork was complete.

I saw Frank one more time. His wife and children's annual visit to Texas, and my new openness with David, freed us finally to spend more than the brief snatched weekends we had endured over the past year. I booked my children into an Upstate New York summer camp, figuring I'd see Frank while the boys were in the countryside. The camp calendar required I fly to New York a day early, so I asked Frank if the boys and I might stay at his place for the night. Our meetings always took place in hotel rooms that I paid for. This was his opportunity to pay me back.

'Do you really think it's a good idea?' he asked, reminding me that my children still did not know about the two of us.

I figured we could be discreet and, since it would save me about $300, I thought, yes, it was a great idea. But I told him I'd book a hotel if he felt it wasn't.

'No, no,' he assured me. 'It's fine. The apartment is empty except for me anyway. The boys can take the bunk beds; you can have our, er, *my* bed; and I'll sleep on the sofa. I'll find a way to fuck you.'

In retrospect it was a lunatic idea. I saved money, but it cost me the relationship. We had acted out our fantasies in a number of romantic hotel rooms. Now we'd be dealing with reality.

I was confident the care and originality Frank put into his tattoo would be reflected in his home. I was wrong. His apartment building was a red-brick tower on an anonymous block like so many others in Queens. Besides some of his wife's paintings on the walls, domestic touches were minimal. There was no dining room, and the only table I saw was in the entry hall and wasn't large enough to seat all four members of his family at once. The kitchen was tiny and betrayed no evidence anyone there cooked. In the master bedroom was a white dressing table and a queen-sized bed with a blue padded headboard pushed into a corner. The furniture was in the same style as the plastic pieces I used to play with in my early-1970s Barbie Dream House. I did not feel like Barbie there, and I was not in a Dream House.

How could a successful Manhattan lawyer live like this? I wondered. And what kind of woman would tolerate it?

It shouldn't matter how someone you love decorates their world. Yet my professional life revolves around selling people's image, and I was stunned by what I saw. I knew it was a superficial reaction, that I was being a judgemental bitch, but the visuals provoked me to reconsider the man.

In the middle of the night Frank crept into my room and we made love, slowly and silently, so as not to disturb the children. It was good to be in his arms again. I was having my period, just as on our first night together, and some blood ended up on the sheets. Months later Frank told me he could still see a faint stain even after he'd washed the sheets a dozen times.

The next morning, while on the bus together en route to the boys' camp, I realised it was more pleasant to be on a cramped bus than inside Frank's apartment. The bus ride back to the city was an even better experience. Frank put his coat across both our laps, and I gave him a hand-job. Until the woman sitting behind us interrupted us and suggested we move to the rear of the bus, I was back in fantasy land.

Then we took the subway back to Frank's place for dinner. He had promised to cook, having said, in one of our phone conversations, 'I know how to make a mean spaghetti.' I looked forward to a romantic dinner for two.

Standing in the kitchen, I watched him boil a pot of water and then throw in some dry spaghetti. After ten minutes he grabbed a jar of marinara sauce from the cupboard, heated it, then poured the sauce over the drained pasta that was sitting in the pot. He took two paper plates out of their cellophane wrapper and served the spaghetti, along with a slice of cold Italian bread.

'What happened to your real plates?' I asked.

'What do you mean?' he said. 'These are real plates.'

To me, paper plates are for barbecues. 'Don't you have china plates, Frank?'

'No, this is it,' he said casually, oblivious.

I later told Bernadette about the paper plates. 'Maybe he and his wife had an argument about doing the washing-up, and decided the only way to solve the dispute was to eat off paper plates,' she said. 'Did he use plastic cutlery as well?'

A later boyfriend, Daniel, pointed to the paper plates as proof that internet relationships were a sham – glorified one-night stands. 'How can a Jewish girl like you, who thinks about food as often as she thinks about sex, hang out with a guy who doesn't understand the importance of china plates?' he asked. His evidence was pretty damning. 'You can't sponge up sauce with the bread, because it soaks into the paper. They go all bendy and damp, like a limp cock, when anything wet is placed on them. Only a guy who doesn't like food would eat off paper plates all the time. Face it, Suz, it's not normal. You didn't love Paper-plate Man.'

Daniel was right. In the real world, Frank and I would have been a one-off, and I would have been telling my friends about a guy I'd met who ate off paper plates. Perhaps it was the paper plates that brought me back to earth. Or perhaps it was the gradual realisation that – way out of practice after so many years off the market – I'd overestimated Frank. I'd spent fifteen months projecting my own fantasies on to him, but on that last trip to New York I learnt how set in his ways Frank was, and how trapped.

I had to admit to myself that he was never going to leave his wife, and I was never going to move to New York. I also had to admit I had been watching the calendar. In a few months my divorce would come through, and I'd become increasingly conscious that soon I would be free to see single men anywhere in the world and would never have to sneak around again. I loved Frank, but my feelings had evolved into a different kind of love – one based on gratitude, perhaps. I had invested great hope and imagination into the affair, but the truth was different. Ultimately Frank proved a disappointment. For a while, particularly during our online courtship, he was what I wanted him to be. But the reality didn't live up to my expectations. He had taught me to think of myself as desirable, though. And he had reawakened my sexuality. His gift to me was confidence, and that's what I used to throw myself back into my single life.

4. SINGING FOR MY SUPPER

The day my husband moved out, my au pair moved in. His name was Josef; he was a nineteen-year-old from Slovakia, and adorable – but, then, he was a teenager and so many of them are. He had short brown hair, was about 5'10" and showed signs of a fit body under his Bratislava T-shirt. God, I thought, I'd forgotten how adorable a nineteen-year-old can be. Not that I thought about fucking him – he was, after all, my employee, here to take care of my two sons, not me – but I wondered if my eyes betrayed my appreciation since he looked scared shitless. Maybe it was that Josef wasn't expecting the mother of his new charges to meet him at Victoria Coach Station in a miniskirt and a pair of four-inch Sergio Rossi heels. Or maybe it was that he was completely incapable of communicating.

I soon discovered, as I attempted to explain the day's busy schedule, that Josef's English was minimal. Using the simplest language I could muster, I explained that movers were coming, my ex-husband was moving out and the kids would be spending the night at their father's new flat. I left out the part about the guy who'd be coming by later that night to cook me dinner and fuck me for dessert. Some things are best left unsaid. The boy had only just landed in the UK and I didn't want him running back to the station to hop on the next bus to Eastern Europe.

Josef was the focus of my day; Søren, the focus of my night. He was a gorgeous Danish chef I'd met two weeks earlier at a party celebrating the relaunch of the Hempel in Bayswater, formerly a dowdy, traditional hotel that the designer Anouska Hempel had transformed into a cool, minimalist Zen retreat.

Søren was the only good-looking straight guy there. I spotted him standing by the right side of the bar while I was crossing the lobby for another free cocktail. I was on the other side of the room but thought it worth squeezing through the fashionistas and liggers to get to the other side.

As I got closer I saw he was wearing Levi 501s and a white button-down shirt that blended with the all-white interior. He was tall and very fit, his muscular legs straining the seams at the thighs. The five-o'clock shadow lent character to his round face and, with his clipped blond hair and radiant blue eyes, he looked like the cover of an A-ha album.

When I got next to him, I said the first thing that came into my mind. 'God knows what they put in these things. They're lethal.'

'Yes, I know,' he said in a charming accent. 'I am on my third of these things.'

I was on my third, too, but chose not to share this information.

Mine wasn't the most brilliant chat-up line, but it worked. Soon we were standing together in a corner, leaning against the walls and getting smashed on raspberry martinis.

He said he was a chef at a West End restaurant called the Sugar Club. I knew it – a fash place where getting a table meant enduring a three-month waiting list if not privy to the secret number reserved for VIP guests. He also had a lucrative sideline, he said, concocting private dinner parties for a middle-aged gay man in Kensington who liked the idea of being served by a beefy blond in tight jeans and a tight T-shirt.

'Sometimes I let him slap my ass. I get a bigger tip,' he said. 'It means nothing. I like girls.'

I could tell. His sentences were short but his body talked plenty.

His dream was to run a bakery. Cooking was a pleasure, he said, but baking was his passion. I knew he had to be an excellent chef to score a job at a top London restaurant. Diners want good food; they don't care, or even know, if the chef's biceps bulge tastily as he grinds steak tartare in the kitchen.

I asked him his name.

'Søren.'

'Excuse me?'

'Søren.'

'Well, I really think you're going to have to change that, for a start,' I said. 'How do you expect to become a famous baker if people can't pronounce your name?'

By midnight I was as drunk as I was going to allow myself to get, at least on a school night, so I got right to the point. 'I'm sorry, but I really must kiss you,' I said.

Before he had a chance to respond I had my tongue in his mouth, and that was the start of our relationship.

The great thing about going out with someone who cooks is that I don't have to. My ex-husband couldn't boil an egg, so when it comes to seeking out new partners I tend to look for the things I missed out on during my marriage – cooking, oral sex, two-way conversations.

Søren rang me three days later and we arranged to meet at Soho House, a members-only club popular with media folk and actors. I drank four vodka martinis, straight up with an olive, then offered to drive him home to the flat in Notting Hill he shared with friends. I was wearing spray-on black PVC trousers. Whether it was the martinis or hormones, I was feeling frisky. My hot Danish pastry couldn't come back to my place because this was not one of my kids-free nights; his place was out because I didn't fancy meeting his flatmates – I wanted to fuck, not fraternise.

I pulled the car over on Ladbroke Grove, a fairly busy main street connecting Holland Park to the Harrow Road. And then I unbuttoned his fly.

I tried pulling my trousers off in the car but, between the PVC, my body heat and the tight fit, they weren't budging. So I opened the car door, stepped into the road and peeled them off there. Then we carried on.

I'd never had sex in a car before, so had to learn where the most comfortable positions were. I quickly discovered there really aren't any in a VW Golf cabriolet. Eventually, we figured out that, by tilting the seats all the way back, I could straddle his legs without hitting my head on the roof. We fucked that way for a half-hour, oblivious to any people walking by. Soon enough our hot breath steamed the windows, ensuring a privacy of sorts. Søren came; I didn't, but that was hardly surprising, since one of my knees was jammed against the seatbelt holder and the steering wheel was pressed into my back. It was painful, but I chose to ignore it at the time.

The next morning I rang up Søren and we compared bruises, the souvenirs of our previous night's romp.

Søren said, 'I have weird marks on my thigh.'

'I know what you mean,' I said. 'This morning, in the bathroom mirror, I saw the imprint of the steering wheel on my back. In black and blue. Maybe next time we could go somewhere a bit more comfortable?'

Our first night together taught me two things: first, a VW Golf is just too small for sex; second, drinking four vodka martinis leads to reckless behaviour and pain. I shared these revelations with Søren, who told me that, on a scale of one to ten, the experience rated an eight. Not bad for a first date and enough to guarantee a second.

A few days later, the movers were carting off the last of my ex-husband's things and, while the sexy new au pair was upstairs unpacking his bags, I was having a dinner date at my place – with my date doing the cooking. Other than Frank's 'homemade' pasta meal, this was the first time in ten years I'd been at home and not had to cook for someone else. Not being on duty was ecstasy.

Søren showed up promptly at seven, again in tight 501s and a tight white T-shirt, carrying not just the food but all the cooking equipment he needed as well. I sat on my worktop, dressed in a denim skirt (no knickers) and a tight T-shirt, and watched him cook. He began chopping the vegetables quickly and skilfully, just like I'd seen chefs do on cookery programmes, but which I'd never been able to emulate myself without spending the dinner hour at the A&E. I found it incredibly horny – not so much watching him cook as witnessing the confidence with which he handled himself.

He had many talents in the kitchen, another of which was the way he smoothly lifted my skirt, pushed down his jeans and fucked me on the worktop, all while waiting for the fish stock to reduce. His timing was impeccable – he came when the stock was ready. He's the only man I've ever met who can keep one eye on the stove, the other on me, and still maintain a hard-on. Some men *can* multitask.

After pulling out, Søren finished preparing the dinner – a four-star trout-on-rocket salad – and, after we'd eaten, cleared the plates and washed the dishes, too. Even if I hadn't had sex that night, it would have ranked as one of my more memorable dates. My au pair benefited, as well. Søren prepared an extra plate for Josef, whom I suspect was as much cowering as unpacking and watching TV upstairs in the loft, having seen my ex-husband move out, my kids disappear and me welcome a lover, all on his first day in a new country.

While Josef stayed out of sight, Søren and I went straight from dinner to dessert – in my bedroom. The dessert was anticlimactic. Søren was a great kisser and a spectacular cook, but I discovered he didn't like to eat pussy. Frank had spoilt me. After sucking Søren's cock for an hour, I began to suspect he was not going to reciprocate.

'Please lick my pussy,' I begged.

He didn't answer but soon manoeuvred into the same position most men take when they don't want to comply with that request – the missionary position.

The next morning I called Bernadette. 'Is it normal for guys not to eat pussy on the second date?' I asked.

'Ewww,' she said, disgusted. 'Do you really like that?'

As I hung up the phone, my mother called.

'Hey, want some bread?' I said. I told her I was dating a baker and that he had given me a half-dozen loaves. I told her he really knew his stuff.

'Great,' she said, not hugely enthusiastic. 'Now all you need is a butcher and a candlestick maker, and you'll be all set.'

I decided not to pursue the oral-sex question.

I still needed a second opinion, so later that day, between crunches at Crunches, I sussed out my personal trainer, Anne Marie.

'Give it time,' she said. 'Maybe he doesn't want to give away all his party tricks at once.'

I wondered if that was how guys really thought. 'I always give away *my* party tricks on the first or second date,' I said. 'I don't see the point of holding back. Anyway, something tells me he's not going to be around that long.'

I explained that Søren was opening his own bakery in a couple of weeks and that our schedules would be in total conflict; he'd be going to bed around the time I'd be coming home from the office.

'In a good relationship,' said Anne Marie, 'people can always work around the conflicts.'

'Well, we still have to sort out the not-eating-pussy issue,' I reminded her. 'So we'll see.'

Søren managed to see me every couple of weeks, but what *I* saw was that our relationship just wasn't working.

I'd call. 'Hi, Søren. This is Suzanne calling. It would be great to see you again. Give me a ring when you can.'

It would be days before he returned a message. As predicted, Søren's hours and mine were indeed incompatible. The new bakery took up all of his waking and too many of his sleeping-around hours. More than once, a date we put in our diaries got postponed.

'Hi, Suzanne. I cannot see you tonight. My oven broke. I have to wait here. The repair guy is coming.'

We'd reschedule.

'Hi, Søren, this is Suzanne calling. *Again*. It would be great to see you. *Again*. Give me a ring when you can.'

I came to the conclusion it wasn't worth waiting for a man who, when he did show, was totally exhausted and fell asleep as soon as he got in bed. This isn't working, I found myself thinking. Why wait for a man who won't even go down on me?

Still, Søren's dinners almost compensated for the frustration, so I continued to leave messages on his mobile phone – and continued to get delayed replies. More than once I found myself wondering if he was simply trying to blow me off, and thinking maybe I was too stupid to take the hint. And then I'd receive a message from Søren saying he hoped to see me soon.

'Hey, Suzanne. I got your messages. Sorry I have not been in touch. I am so busy with the bakery. But let us keep in touch.'

Let's not, I thought. Good guy, bad timing. I called the bakery, his real mistress, and left a message whose short sentences Søren was sure to understand. 'Hi, Søren. Suzanne here. Tired of calling. Good luck with the business. Bye.'

It was time to move on. I hadn't gone online since meeting Frank and had fallen out of the habit. I was too old for hanging out in singles bars and nightclubs, too old for dressing up, putting on make-up and standing around all night hoping to meet guys, like I had done in my youth. Meeting Søren at a hotel party was a fluke. I was ready to try something new.

One afternoon at work, while scanning the papers for references to my clients, I turned a page and saw the personal ads. I briefly contemplated the wisdom of placing one of my own.

I was not a virgin to the personals, but my only other experiences had taken place so many years earlier and had proved so disappointing, I didn't hold out much hope. Shortly after losing my virginity, I answered two intriguing ads in *Time Out*. My first date sounded artistic and promised romance, but turned out to be a drunk in St John's Wood who groped me, then passed out on his bathroom floor while going to the toilet; relieved, I walked out of the flat and left him there. The second date took place after my school friend Kelly and I responded, for a laugh, to a hilarious ad.

Two Warlocks, Young, Attractive, Seek Two Witches to Spellbind Them.

We arranged to meet at the Windsor Castle, a pub in Maida Vale then frequented by punks. By the time they arrived – two guys in their early twenties, one a rockabilly stud, the other an emaciated punk with chipped black teeth – Kelly and I had been waiting forty-five minutes and had downed two pints of lager each. Another two pints later, the guys invited us back to their flat on what turned out to be Warlock Road. Oh, I get it! I remember thinking. How clever!

We all smoked a joint, then the boys asked us to tie them to the double bed. Oh, 'bind'. Like 'spellbind'. I get it! That revelation didn't click in till much later, alas, after I'd thought back on that night. At the time, I was so drunk I didn't consider this request particularly unusual and, conveniently, ropes had already been tied to the bedpost to make it easier. So I tied them up. Then I sucked on the rockabilly's cock for a while, until I found his elbow and, in my stoned haze, licked that for a half-hour, thinking I'd found a new erogenous zone.

Eventually, I looked up and I noticed Kelly had done a runner, leaving me alone with two strangers. 'I have to go now,' I said, and fled, leaving them to pull a Houdini. I figured the knots were loose enough that they could escape easily. And they were. The next day Mr Broken Teeth, the one I'd ignored, rang me up to say how much they'd both enjoyed meeting me and suggested another date. I opted out of the personals for two and a half decades.

After calling it off with Søren, I wrote up an ad and placed it in the *Guardian* and the *Independent*, the two arty left-wing papers I read, hoping to attract a few arty left-wing guys.

Sexy, smart, fit, funny American media chick, 41, seeks handsome, successful man, fit, funny, 38–50, for lightweight relationship.

I got thirty-two responses from the *Guardian* and whittled them down; I put the twenty-five responses from the *Independent* aside to save for a later date. After listening to my messages, I deleted anyone whose voice was too high or too cockney. I also nixed anyone whose job sounded boring and anyone who lived south of the river. After the frustrations of my long-distance relationship with Frank, I decided never to go out with anyone who lived more than five miles from home. That left seventeen possibilities – enough dates to keep me in dinners for the next three months.

Though he hadn't worked out, my Great Dane had spoilt me. He had a good body and a deep voice, and dinners with him had been a real treat. I hoped to find his replacement.

Johnny did not sound like a *Guardian* reader as he spoke in monosyllables. I didn't get the feeling he read much at all. But he said he was a thirty-eight-year-old builder from Scotland and lived nearby in Cricklewood. Potentially hot. He also mentioned that he looked like Antonio Banderas, and was just looking for some fun. *Definitely* hot. For the first time since college, I decided to break my golden rule and meet a man whose voice I didn't like. When you look like Antonio Banderas, certain things, including an incomprehensible Glaswegian accent, are forgivable. He may not have sounded very intelligent, but he did live almost within walking distance, and, I discovered, he *did* look like Antonio Banderas.

We had a quick first meet to check out the goods at a local wine bar a few hundred metres from my house. When I walked in I recognised him right away. I was wearing drainpipe jeans and a sweatshirt; he was wearing broad shoulders, meaty biceps and the same triangular shape as my boys' action figure toys.

He had a Foster's and I ordered a glass of Chardonnay. 'Do you actually read the *Guardian*?' I asked.

'Not really,' he admitted. 'I read the *Guide*. I like the listings. You know, what's on in the movies, that kind of thing.'

'Do you read any newspaper?'

'No. What's the point? It's always the same old shit. Politicians, natural disasters, sports. Boring.'

It's hard to maintain a conversation with someone who makes English – his native tongue – sound like a foreign language. Still, Johnny was cute and local. After an hour, I got the sense it wasn't going to work out with my movie star, so we both moved towards the door.

'Do you have a car?' I asked.

'No, I'm walking.'

I offered to give him a lift.

We got in my car and were outside his door in five minutes. His flat, just off the A41, in the back of someone's garden, looked more like a garage than a residence.

'Do you want to come in?' he asked.

I told him I couldn't stay for long, that I had to be up early to take my kids to school. That didn't seem to bother him.

He opened the door and we walked into a large mostly vacant room. There was a makeshift table just inside the door that held a computer. A small sofa faced a telly just beyond that and, on the other side of a half-wall divider, there was a double bed, still unmade. A tiny bathroom was off a far wall. I don't recall seeing a kitchen.

I felt awkward. I didn't see a chair and didn't know if I should remain standing or sit down on the sofa or the bed. Johnny pointed to the sofa, solving my dilemma, and said, 'Do you want to watch some television?'

'Not really,' I said. 'I'm not really here to watch television.' So I kissed him.

He leant into me and steered me towards the bed. He was incredibly keen – a bit too keen. There wasn't much foreplay; there wasn't much of anything, sadly. When I looked down from the perfect pecs, broad shoulders and bulging biceps, what I saw down there was so small it might as well not have been there.

I figured doggy style was the only position that would facilitate my feeling anything, so, like an obedient dog, I got on all fours. Johnny put on a condom – I hated myself for noticing how it was too big for the job – and entered me from behind. I think. It was hard to tell whether he was in or out. It was hard to tell if he was hard. If the average white cock doubles in size when erect, then his, hard, would have been about two inches long. I thought anal might be the answer.

Employing my most seductive voice, I said, 'Can you slip your cock in my ass?'

He moved into position and probed my butt. Again I couldn't feel a thing. Again it was disappointing. I couldn't imagine Antonio Banderas with a two-inch cock. Funny, his self-declared lookalike hadn't mentioned that particular detail before our first date. Nothing was working for me, but at least Johnny was satisfied.

After he came, I said, 'Listen, I'd better be going. You're only around the corner. Let's meet up again sometime.'

'Just let me know. You know where I am.'

Normally I wouldn't have considered a second date with a man whose distinction was having the smallest cock I'd ever seen, but a few weeks later I got an invitation to a private party at Opium, a fashionable West End club, and needed a chaperone. A friend handling the event said there would be free shots and canapés.

'Free drinks?' said Johnny. 'Sounds great. Count me in.'

I invited Johnny not so much for sex – after our first date, I wasn't sure I wanted to go back there again – but I didn't fancy going to the party on my own and figured he'd make a good chaperone, as long as he didn't open his mouth.

The barman passed out small bottles filled with a spirit containing a prune at the bottom. He told us it was Japanese, one hundred per cent proof – and on the house.

'There you go, then,' I said to Johnny. 'I'm going to see if there's anyone here I know. Are you OK?'

'You don't have to worry about me,' he said, knocking back his first shot. 'I'll be fine.'

I left Johnny to enjoy the freebies, while I networked with some fellow PR people I recognised. As I walked towards the familiar faces, a cute black boy stopped me and said, 'Is that Agent Provocateur perfume you're wearing?'

I told him it was.

'I'd follow a woman with that scent anywhere.'

Nice line, but he was too young to be fuck material. We had a dance anyway, before I moved on.

I walked back to the bar several times to check on Johnny and found him knocking back the shots. Later, when I realised it was well after midnight, I went back for the last time. 'Do you mind if we leave?' I asked.

I got our coats while Johnny went to the toilet. We agreed to meet by the bar.

Twenty minutes later, it was apparent he wasn't going to.

I peeked my head into the men's loo. 'Johnny? Are you in there?'

A cubicle opened and Johnny stepped out, stripped down to his boxers.

'What are you doing without your clothes on? *Where* are your clothes?'

'My clothes?' he said, not comprehending.

'Yes. Your clothes. The things you wear. Where are they?'

He looked down. 'Oh. Shit.'

A bouncer appeared at the door. 'Excuse me, madam, but ladies can't use the men's toilet.'

I told him I didn't want to use the men's toilet and explained the situation. Then I asked him to help my friend.

As the bouncer entered the toilet, I saw Johnny thrust his hands up above his head. 'It's OK! It's OK! You can take me in!' he screamed, apparently mistaking the bouncer for a cop.

I waited another ten minutes and still no Johnny. I drove home alone. This was one Banderas movie I did not want to see again.

There were sixteen other dates on my *Guardian* list but, after my experience with an alcoholic with a cock the size of my thumb, I went instead to the list of *Independent* readers I'd put aside.

I chose a man named Giles because he sounded fascinating. He had published several novels and seemed glamorous and highbrow and nice. He also had the poshest accent I'd ever heard. Like me, he was divorced, in his forties and had two kids. He lived in the middle of nowhere, in the Wye Valley, three hours west of London, but said his work frequently brought him to the city. After my experience with Frank, I should have disqualified him purely on the basis of location, but I was wary of having another two-inch Johnny just down the road. Plus, Giles told me he lived in a cottage, which sounded charming and romantic as he described it in emails. He said he kept the house warm with log fires. I pictured a man making his own candles in a cosy stone kitchen. If things work out, I thought, it could be the perfect weekend getaway. That fantasy was cut short during our second telephone call when his sweater caught fire and he had to hang up quickly.

During our third phone conversation, Giles told me he had two tickets for an opera at the Coliseum and invited me to join him. He suggested dinner before the show. A double bill! I thought, quite pleased at the prospect.

'May I have a kiss first,' he asked, 'so we can get that part over with?'

Before consenting, I made Opera Man work for it. I emailed a survey I devised just for him, with questions about the car he drove and the alcohol he drank, his star sign, his dress sense, the kind of clothes he liked on women, his favourite way to kiss. He took the challenge, writing he'd once had his chart done 'by a woman who used a computer rather than a crystal ball' and had discovered he was 'a typical Sagittarius'. I took that to mean a free spirit who liked to travel, hopefully in my direction. He described his dress sense as 'tending to the extravagant' to the point where his daughter called him a 'straight gay man'. Like every man I've known, he had a thing for high-heeled shoes on women and, like too many men, drove a Range Rover. He drank gin and white wine, as did I. He didn't answer the question about the kiss. Still, he sounded like a smarty and, following Johnny, who was a virtual illiterate, that was just what I wanted.

We arranged to meet at the Pizza Express on St Martin's Lane. It wouldn't have been my first choice for a dinner, being neither particularly expensive nor exclusive. I supposed Giles's rationale was that it was both local to the theatre and cheap. Still, that worried me a bit. If a guy suggests Pizza Express as a first date, he's probably thinking that, if I turn out to be a dud, he won't have wasted too much money – that is, assuming he pays. Unless it's a first date, I normally have my wallet out so fast it's like I'm practising for a gunslinging scene in a Hollywood Western, while secretly hoping the guy says, 'This one's on me.'

I spotted Giles immediately in the crowded restaurant. As promised, he was wearing a black fedora. I thought that an arty touch; so few men wear hats of any kind any more. He took off the hat, tossed his wavy shoulder-length brown hair and stood to greet me. I saw he was slim, of medium height and medium build and quite good-looking, in a bohemian sort of way. His sweet face and brown eyes offset his black trousers and baggy black turtleneck – very old-school thespian, the kind of man one would expect to see in a cape.

Not knowing what was or wasn't appropriate attire for an opera, I'd dressed a bit thespian myself, Barbara Stanwyck manqué – black pencil skirt, tight-fitting pink blouse, high heels, plus a short brown mohair jacket and a matching brown fedora of my own. I felt very film noir.

The real darkness was still ahead. I found my first opera, Stravinsky's *The Rake's Progress*, long, boring and difficult, a discomfiting orgy of minor chords. I managed to get through it without falling asleep, however, all the while thinking, If I'm going to sleep in this curious man's presence, it won't be here.

During the interval Giles had kissed me. He had bad breath – strike one. Still, we kissed some more after the show, bad breath being a small price to pay for getting laid, I figured. His kisses, though not unpleasant, weren't like Frank's or Søren's and didn't make my head go fuzzy. Back in the theatre, Giles had manoeuvred his hand on to my thigh, moving up my skirt during the performance until he was practically rubbing my pussy. He had paid for dinner and now I wondered if this was the price I had to pay for the opera ticket. At least it kept me awake.

Afterwards, as Giles knew a member of the cast, we went backstage and met the lead baritone. 'Suzanne has never been to the opera before,' Giles said as an introduction, laughing as he spilled the secret I'd foolishly shared over dinner. His tone implied I'd led an uncultured existence all the years before this attempt at civilising me. I didn't like it; I hadn't expected him to patronise me or use my secret against me.

After the opera and backstage visit, Giles took me to his room at the Holiday Inn Bloomsbury. It was extremely tiny – barely enough room for the double bed and the minibar. He had bought two mini bottles of champagne – bigger ones wouldn't have fitted in the room's fridge – and put them on ice after checking in before the theatre. The champagne was cold – nice touch – we had a drink and started messing around.

I undid his trousers and kissed him. Then I put my mouth around his cock. He came instantly – strike two.

'Good heavens!' he said. 'I'm so sorry I came so fast.'

'It's OK,' I lied. I didn't know what else to say. I felt a little embarrassed for him and quite disappointed for myself. I'd got all worked up, all for five minutes of foreplay. It seemed appropriate to move on to safer terrain. 'Thanks for the opera. It was interesting,' I lied. 'I wasn't expecting the music to be quite so ... dissonant. I prefer something with a bit more melody.'

'Yes, me, too,' he agreed, game to the derailment. He congratulated me on staying awake, saying, perhaps for my benefit, 'I know opera buffs who'd have fallen asleep during that performance.'

He moved towards me and we kissed again. I hoped he was planning to redeem himself on Round Two. I could see he was hard again, so I climbed on top of him. He came within five minutes.

'Do you ever talk dirty?' I asked, thinking, My turn to be aroused. I rather fancied a man with a posh accent talking dirty to me: the contrast between highbrow and low, posh and filth was horny.

'Dirty?' he said.

'Yeah, dirty,' I said. 'You know, like, "I'd really like to lick your cunt" or "Fuck me hard". That sort of thing.'

'Oh, my God. No! I couldn't possibly say anything like that.'

I was making him nervous. Very nervous and uncomfortable.

'What? Never? Ever? You've never said "Suck my cock"?'

'Never! If I said anything like that, it would come out sounding positively medical.'

He hadn't made me come. He didn't want to talk dirty. He had bad breath. I contemplated calling a cab, but instead suggested he let me sit on his face. 'Do you mind?' I asked, manoeuvring towards him. I didn't really give him a chance to answer. The score was 0–2 – zero hits, two strikes – and, given the tally, I thought it a fair request.

Giles looked horrified. Either he'd never met a woman who'd communicated what *she* wanted in bed, or he was appalled at the idea of cunnilingus. I didn't much care either way. Clearly, this was going to be a one-off; there'd be no rematch and I was determined to score at least one point. So, before calling off the whole game, I mounted his face.

If I were a hooker, it would have been fine that he'd made no effort to satisfy me. A hooker's services are designed to facilitate a man's getting off; that's the job they're paid to do. But I wasn't being paid and I'm not a hooker. We'd been email buddies for a few weeks and spent a few hours chatting on the phone. I had even entertained the fantasy that my correspondence with this charming, learned man might lead to a regular gig. Now we'd been for dinner, to the opera and to bed, and I just wanted to get off and go home. I didn't give a shit if he liked oral sex or not. I figured I'd grind on his face and have my own orgasm within five minutes. Instead of accepting strike three, I rubbed my clit against his lips and came almost as quickly as he had. Then I told him I'd go downstairs and get a cab home.

The following day, I felt blue about my night with Giles. Despite his patronising attitude at the opera, our email and telephone conversations prior to then were fun and seemed promising. Had we not had sex, our growing friendship might have grown into something permanent. But I did not believe this was a man who could be trained. A man either likes oral sex or he doesn't. A man either likes talking dirty or he doesn't. Some sexual preferences, I concluded, really do emerge in black and white. I had tried turning an uncomfortable bedmate into something he was not. I felt awful about forcing my tastes on to this nice man.

The clash in the way we expressed our sexual needs had been so great I feared it had created a divide between us.

A few days after our tryst, I rang Giles. 'I'm sorry about what happened in the hotel room,' I said. 'We're obviously sexually incompatible, and it makes me feel sad, because until that night I was really enjoying our friendship.'

'I'm so glad you rang, Suzanne. I've been feeling low, too.' Giles said that, in the days between our last meeting and my phone call, he'd been walking around in a funk, feeling out of sorts. 'I couldn't put my finger on what was wrong, but, being with you in that hotel room, it just didn't feel right.'

I suggested we rewind the tape and pretend our episode in the hotel never happened. We went back to being email buddies, and I went back to Nerve.

5. MEDIA MAN

I can't say I developed a preference for an *Independent* man over a *Guardian* man. Of my admittedly small sample of two, one had a small cock; the other didn't know how to use his.

I wasn't short on potential dates. The newspapers ran my ad gratis the second week when they saw how successful my first had been. When I rang to check messages there were another thirty or so personals to sort through. Almost a year's worth of dinners, should I ever go hungry, I thought.

I invested a couple of months in going down the list, all ending in disaster for one reason or another. There was the boring guy with the boring job who spent an hour describing his IT support company; he made me want to go to sleep – alone. There was the guy who worked as a 'relationship manager' for Barclays; he spent so much time explaining why the bank no longer referred to people in this position as bank managers, I knew our own relationship would never get off the ground. There was the guy who drove his BMW so slowly I wanted to get out and push it; that date went nowhere fast. Then there was the impoverished artist who took me to his one-man show and then, after learning I was a publicist, tried to score PR services for free; he did not score with me.

Taking out personals in newspapers did not prove as successful as I'd hoped. Following up on the responses was a diversion from looking after my kids and running a busy company, not to mention a way of passing the time between my current date and the promise of a keeper. But mostly I wished I'd been passing the time some other way.

Then, at my office Christmas party at Soho House, I hooked up with Lance. He was the editor of a lads' mag and a notorious cad around town. I was standing against the wall, talking to a member of my staff as we sipped post-dinner nightcaps in the Circle Bar. I recognised Lance from previous visits to the club and from parties we'd both attended. I nodded in recognition; he nodded back. I'd had four Belvedere martinis and was drunk, and, when Lance stumbled across the room and stuck his tongue down my throat, I realised he was, too. From what I could tell, pretty much everyone in the Circle Bar was that night.

I'd always found Lance quite sexy. He wasn't more than 5'9", was stocky and broad shouldered, with short spiky dirty-blond hair. Not standard-issue attractive, but he had presence and was arrogant, and somehow I found that swoon-worthy. Plus, he looked like a young Rod Stewart.

He said nothing, just kept kissing me. I didn't stop him, despite being in the presence of my employees. Plus, Lance was a good kisser, so I let him continue, and hoped my staff was too wrecked to notice, or remember, when Lance pushed me against the wall, slipped his hand under my blouse, and pulled down my bra to cop a feel. The room was noisy and people were in high spirits. So was I. I was excited he was so filthy. About fucking time. A fellow pervert.

That night, when I went home to bed, alone, I wondered if Lance fucked as well as he kissed. The next week I called him up on a work matter. We'd been in contact regarding one of my clients, a soap-opera star whom he wanted for a centrefold. Since it would have meant wearing a bikini, I'd rung the actress's agent, who vetoed the idea. I rang Lance to tell him the idea wouldn't fly. 'I think you owe me some kind of compensation, Suzanne, don't you?'

'Compensation? Like dinner, you mean?'

'Dinner sounds good,' he said.

'How about Saturday, then? I'll book a table and let you know.'

'You're on.'

His flirtatious tone implied he was expecting more than dinner, and so was I, so I booked a table at Odette's, a romantic dimly lit French restaurant in Primrose Hill. Lance arrived on time. The French waiter sat us at a small table for two against a wall that separated the large dining room from our more intimate alcove. Reproductions of vintage French posters covered the walls, which were painted a pale lemon. We both ordered the fillet steak, accompanied by a good bottle of Merlot.

'It must be great to be the big boss of a men's magazine,' I said.

'Yeah, it's been fun,' he admitted. 'But I've been doing it for a while and I'm thinking about my next move.'

'What's next?'

'Simply put, I want to be famous.'

'How so?' I asked. 'Well known in the industry or, like, everyone-knows-who-you-are kind of famous?'

'I want everyone to know my name.'

'But you already are quite well known,' I protested. 'You've been on TV, you have the magazine ...'

He told me he wanted to write a book. 'I've already got the title: *Six Months to Find a Wife*. I want to do the personals, go online, visit speed-dating clubs, that kind of thing. And then write about it, you know?'

Yes, I thought, I know that kind of thing a little too well. I was also thinking his ambition to be nothing but famous was shallow. And that he was ten times better than any of my personal-ad dates. I suspected Lance wouldn't have to do much research before he landed the woman of his dreams.

After dinner I suggested we find some place for a coffee, as I knew he lived near by. Then when we stepped outside I used my favourite line. 'I really must kiss you now.'

'You're so obvious, Suzanne,' he said, smiling.

We were back at his place in fifteen minutes.

It was a grim basement flat in the back end of Camden Town. There were no curtains, no tables or chairs or furniture of any kind except a worn sofa and a widescreen TV. It reminded me of the student hovels I'd seen while at university. I'd expected better from a man with a posh accent who edited a magazine that featured the occasional interior-decoration spread.

Either they're not paying him enough or it's all going up his nose, I thought. I ignored the dishes spilling over the sink and the fussy floral-patterned duvet cover and matching pillow-cases I spotted through the bedroom door. Let's hope that's a gift from his grandmother.

Since Lance could kiss, I chose to overlook his lack of home furnishings and taste. I straddled him on the sofa, then quickly pulled my top over my head.

'What are you doing?' he shouted.

'I'm taking my top off,' I said, stating the obvious. 'Is there a problem?'

'The neighbours! They might see.'

'I realise that,' I said. 'Surely, that's the point. You don't have curtains on the windows.' For a cad about town, he was being a prude.

He got to his feet and suggested we go to the bedroom. I followed, not bothered one way or another where we went.

We got down to business and it was OK – *just* OK. I sucked his cock for about fifteen minutes; he gave me oral for about three. Then it was on to the usual range of positions: missionary, doggy, him on top, me on top. After about forty-five minutes he hadn't come, and I began to wonder if he was going through the motions like I was. Though his technique was not particularly distinguished, Lance had carved his career out of boasting about the number of women he'd slept with. I was determined, therefore, to give him something he'd remember and most likely didn't get on first dates. I suggested something I figured might get me in his book and would definitely get me going that night.

'Would you like to fuck me up the ass?'

'Wow! Sure!' he said, excited, as though it were the first time a girl had made this suggestion.

'I'll lead,' I said, and I coaxed his cock gently into my ass.

He started to fuck me harder and harder. I could feel he was getting excited, and it was exciting me, too. Finally, my idea of horny.

He shot his spunk in my ass, then pulled out straight after, not pausing to savour the moment, and threw the condom on the floor. 'Wow!' he said. '*That* was a sexual experience!'

Maybe for you, honey, I thought. I still hadn't come.

We went to sleep – well, *he* went to sleep. It was difficult for me to sleep in that rancid flat, and under such a hideous duvet. Plus, Lance snored so loudly I thought he'd wake all of Camden Town. I found the only way to stop the noise was to hold on to his cock. I had never tried this trick before, but it seemed to work. Eventually, my hand got tired, so I rolled over and lay awake, listening.

At daylight I woke up and started masturbating in preparation for morning sex. I knew, if I prepped myself, I'd come this time. Lance hadn't stayed in one position long enough to get me off the previous night. I figured, though, that if he had a man's usual morning hard-on and I mounted him when I was on the verge of coming, he'd satisfy both of us, and think it was all about him.

I pulled it off. We came. Afterwards, we got up to get dressed. His clothes were on the floor, along with the rest of his wardrobe. Mine were in the front room where I'd left them. As I walked towards the door, Lance picked up a book that lay on the floor next to his bed, and, not even looking at it, recited an extract from 'Ode to a Nightingale'. I didn't know if he was trying to be romantic or attempting to prove he wasn't really an insensitive cad about town – something I already knew from the previous night.

My heart aches, and a drowsy numbness pains
My sense, as though of hemlock I had drunk ...

Thank god it's Keats! I thought. The only poetry I remembered from university was the first two lines from 'Ode to a Grecian Urn', which I'd memorised to impress my hot English-lit prof. I wasn't letting Lance get away with that. I didn't want him thinking I was some stupid uncultured American, so I recited a few lines of my own.

Thou still unravish'd bride of quietness,
Thou foster-child of Silence and slow Time ...

He recognised the poem and looked impressed. Mission accomplished. I walked out the door and went home to get some sleep.

6. ONLY LOOKING

It's amazing what you can achieve with a little perseverance and a diet consisting of two meals a day, one of them a hearty bowl of porridge. Having been a stone or two overweight most of my adult life, I finally had the body of my dreams. That is, I was finally a size 12, down from a 16. That's all I ever really wanted – that, and being 5'5" tall. When I was younger I used to dream of reaching 5'5", as I dreaded being as tiny as my mother, my aunt and my grandmother, all of whom hovered around the five-foot mark and had to buy their clothes in the children's department. So, when the prayers paid off and the dreams came true and I managed to reach, and stay, at my target height and weight, I was delighted. I'd had pendulous breasts most of my life and a non-existent squarish ass. The desire to change those things inspired me to stop eating and stay slim. Now, with my new bod, I wanted a permanent monument that celebrated the 'perfect' me. And, if I was going to have photos taken, I thought, why not erotic ones, pictures that showed off my new 38-27-36 figure, toned and shapely butt and perky new tits. So when I spotted a profile on Nerve with the heading 'Models Wanted', I answered it. Since I'd met Frank, Nerve had gone global, or at least had some presence in the UK – although there were only about twenty local guys on it.

One of them was James, and I knew from his first email ours would always be a complicated relationship.

'Sorry!' started one of his earlier notes. 'Just back from Afghanistan, so haven't been on the Net since end of September. E me and we'll see what happens.'

It was already November. At this rate, I wouldn't see him until the new year, and that was a pity – I wanted to show him my new body.

Nerve's personals form was set out like a standardised questionnaire. James described himself as a forty-two-year-old photographer living in London. Beyond that, I knew very little. But his answer to one data point – *Why you should get to know me* – intrigued me: 'I am a sensitive voyeur heavily based in the visual arts. But I'm also an adventurer – riding, flying, skiing, diving and scooting around war zones. I love sex, particularly cunnilingus.'

I thought to myself, If I reply 'I'm a stay-at-home mother of two, heavily based in my home, who occasionally drives to the supermarket but loves cunnilingus,' I probably would not hear back. At least we had one thing in common, though. If I had to choose any form of sex, sitting on someone's face probably ranked alongside, if not above, straightforward fucking. But the rest of his profile didn't make sense to me. It sounded more like a job application than a sex ad.

As I later learnt, he'd been in Afghanistan covering the war for an American news channel. He was their main cameraman. Erotic photography was more a hobby than a full-time career and something he was keen to pursue. I suspected it was an effort to distance himself from some of the gruesome shit he'd seen in his lifetime of covering wars.

I emailed James my number, and he called that evening. I could tell from our conversation that he was everything I didn't want or need. He said he travelled a lot, and, looking through his diary, found one free day in the coming three weeks, then warned that even that date might have to be rescheduled if a disaster struck somewhere and he got assigned to cover it. Like Søren, the baker, he sure didn't keep regular working hours. And, in addition, he was attached. 'I'm kinda married,' he admitted. 'We fuck three times a year, if that. We even have separate rooms.'

'I don't do married,' I said.

He stressed they were more like friends than a couple. He said they led very separate lives. I imagined two people getting drunk from time to time and ending up in the sack. I'd had a relationship like that in my twenties, with a guy I'd moved in with after answering an ad for a flatmate in Boston's alternative weekly, the *Phoenix*. Sometimes, usually after too many shots of Jack Daniels, I would end up on the sofa sucking his dick. The rest of the time he got off with my friends. It was never a comfortable arrangement, because I'd get jealous and wish he were fucking me instead. So I tried to put James off.

'This doesn't sound very good,' I said. 'I'm looking for a steady gig, every Saturday night.'

'I can do phone sex,' he offered.

I told him I didn't want phone sex. 'I've just come out of a relationship with a guy who lived three thousand miles away that was nothing but phone sex. I want real sex now.'

Still, James was insistent. 'Did I tell you how much I love cunnilingus? I'm very good at it, or so I've been told. Perhaps we could meet up and I could eat your pussy all night.'

'Hmmm. Tempting,' I said. He was so persistent, eventually I relented for just one date. 'OK,' I said, 'I give in. Let me know when you're free.'

I next heard from him when he rang from Belfast in the middle of a riot. I heard petrol bombs going off in the background. But I liked his voice, when I could hear it, and liked what I thought he was saying. His voice was low, but gentle and melodic. He had picked up a strange accent during his two decades travelling around the world. With exploding bombs serving as background ambience, I had to fill in the blanks as James attempted to communicate. 'I want to fuck you ... hard ... bursting out ... my pants.'

'I want to fuck you hard'? Or 'I want to suck you. I'm hard'? I couldn't be sure, but, either way, I thought, This is cool – like having sex with the news. 'Where exactly are you right now?' I asked.

'Behind a row of trucks, watching the action. I may have to move in a minute, so, if we get cut off, you'll know why,' he explained. 'What are you wearing?'

I described my sheer blue nightie and peach satin robe. 'You?'

'Very funny. Combats, a jacket and a fucking heavy camera. God, I'd love to be sucking your pussy instead of stuck in this hellhole.'

I pictured him aiming his camera at a group of rioters with one arm, his other arm down his trousers, stroking his cock.

'If this shit finishes up tonight, I'll be back tomorrow. Maybe we can meet up?'

As it turned out, the next day James flew to Edinburgh to cover the Gordon Brown baby story. The UK Chancellor's baby had been born seven weeks premature and died of complications.

I nicknamed James Action Man, even before getting any action from him.

In the space of two weeks, he rang me about six times, always from a different place on the map. I took a sudden interest in watching the television news, knowing he was usually behind the cameras on the lead stories. In between my making him come over the phone and his discussing what kind of erotic photos he wanted to take of me, I told him about my impressive collection of sex toys, something I'd acquired during my time with Frank.

'I'd love to watch you stick a vibrator up your cunt,' he said. 'While I take pictures, of course.'

That could be hot, I thought.

'Or maybe I could film you bent over your kitchen table, in a pair of fuck-me shoes – and nothing else.'

'Sounds great,' I said. 'If we ever meet.'

I warned him that if the dirty phone calls went on much longer, I'd start charging by the minute. I felt like I was providing a service.

'You're my only phone-sex girl,' he said, half-confirming my fears I was providing a service, half-turning me on with compliments. 'Don't worry. We'll meet – *soon*,' he emphasised.

I heard a volcano rumble in the background, then the sat phone went dead. He was in Goma. I liked thinking we might be having the most expensive phone sex ever. News crews use satellite phones when they can't get a mobile signal. At the time, a Goma-to-London call cost $10 a minute. Our virtual sex sessions often lasted thirty minutes.

Still, all this phone sex and no real sex was starting to feel like a bad habit. Even if it was exciting getting the news delivered straight from the man on the scene, I didn't want a fucking phone-sex boyfriend. I wanted a real one, and real fucking.

Finally, two weeks after we first made contact, there was an opening in Action Man's calendar. He called to say he was free the next day, a Tuesday. I told him I couldn't do midweek dates, that Friday and Saturday were my girls' nights out. James was due to fly to Amsterdam on Wednesday, to gather footage for the forthcoming Lockerbie trial. 'I'm really sorry, but it's the only date that I've got,' he said. 'If it's not tomorrow, then it's probably going to be another week till I'm free again, maybe longer.'

'I don't really do this sort of thing,' I protested.

'Are you sure you can't do tomorrow?' he pleaded. 'I'll make it worth your while. I promise.'

He was making me horny, damn him. And my pussy had only had the most perfunctory oral attention since Frank.

'OK,' I relented. 'You've got me. This is a one-time-only midweek special offer.' Then I confirmed Josef, my au pair, was free to take over my domestic duties.

By this time my knickers were wet at the thought of what Action Man and I might do together.

I arranged to meet James at Soho House, and arrived at eight-thirty the next night wearing a short Marc Jacobs denim skirt and blazer, a clingy purple top and matching purple hold-ups. No knickers. My seamless skin-tone bra was so sheer my nipples poked through my top.

He was already there, sitting in the Blue Room, an intimate space off from the main bar. I recognised him from his photo. He was wearing all black – black jeans, black button-down shirt, black blazer. Everyone wears black these days, but on James the black-on-black worked. He was my idea of a spy.

He was over six-feet tall and slim, with slightly receding dark-brown hair, a dark goatee and moustache, and a tan that, had I not known was the result of a job that kept him outdoors all day, I'd have suspected was artificial. He had gentle blue eyes that offset his rugged appearance, and was sexy and masculine and confident enough to order an orange juice from the waitress, as if it were the normal thing to do in a room full of boozers.

'Are you sure you wouldn't prefer to have a drink?' I asked.

He told me he didn't drink. He'd had a few beers when he was a teenager and knew right away it was something he just didn't like. I thought that was refreshing.

For a change, I ordered an orange juice as well, although what I'd really wanted was a Bloody Mary.

James talked about himself a lot, and I thought, When's he going to ask me something? I had just spent two weeks listening to him tell me what he was doing around the globe, and it suddenly occurred to me that he'd never asked about my own work. I wondered if his penis was as big as his ego. The monologue started pissing me off. I was putting more effort into resisting the urge to check my watch than he was putting into me. When he ordered his second orange juice, I took the opportunity to toss a few words into the conversation.

'You look better in the flesh than in that bizarre picture you have on Nerve,' I said. His photo showed him on a mountaintop, standing sideways and dressed in an antique jacket and no trousers. You could see his nice bum in profile. He was holding a sceptre, like he was king of the mountain.

'So do you,' he said. 'A lot better.'

I didn't know if he really believed that, but I liked thinking it might be true. Of course, I'd posted a flattering pic on Nerve, one I felt captured me looking the best I'd ever done in my life. Like his photo, mine was an outside shot. I was wearing an off-the-shoulder peach top and my hair was thrown into a loose braid that fell over one shoulder. I was looking directly into the camera, deliberately inviting. My then husband had taken the photo.

Hmmm, I thought. Maybe something might happen tonight after all.

Then he said, 'Look, I'm really sorry, but I can't stay out late tonight.' He told me he had a seven a.m. flight and had to be up at four. 'When I get back to London, let's get together.'

When will that be? I wondered. This was supposed to be our big date and now he was cutting it short at nine p.m. That's that, I thought – until we stepped out the door onto Greek Street and he grabbed me and pulled my mouth close to his. I gently sucked on his tongue. He put his hands under my coat and up my skirt, and, as he said, 'I really want to lick your pussy,' his fingers began exploring it. Instinctively I pulled him closer, wrapping one leg around him.

Shit! I thought. This is too close to home. Too many of my clients were members of Soho House or worked in the area. Still, I didn't stop him. It felt good to have fingers inside me and risqué to have foreplay on Greek Street. And he knew the terrain.

I could feel his hard-on under his jeans. It turned me on. 'I'll walk you to your car,' he said. He took his fingers out of my pussy and grabbed my hand as we crossed Shaftesbury Avenue and walked to the China Town Car Park. We stopped at the entrance.

'Are you going to leave me here or do you want to see me to my car?' I asked.

My VW Golf cabrio was parked on the first level, ensuring that nearly every car exiting the garage had to pass it. After Søren, I was a little more familiar with the limitations of having sex in my car. Even so, we got in and resumed kissing. I loosened his belt, undid his trousers and tried to mount his rock-hard cock. As always, it wasn't easy climbing over the gearshift.

I guided his cock into my pussy but, just as he was about to enter me, he came. 'Fuck! Sorry!' he said. 'I haven't had sex for a while. That's what happens.'

There goes the prospect of a car fuck, I thought.

Fortunately, James thought otherwise. 'Do these seats recline?'

I showed him how to manoeuvre the handles.

He pushed his seat back until it was horizontal. 'Climb on my face.'

Easier said than done. Because the car was compact, even with the seat reclined I had to play the contortionist to position myself over his smiling face. It wasn't a graceful manoeuvre but I managed to do it, with my elbows resting on the back shelf of the car and my head pushed against the rear window. I put my face down as a token of modesty – it was only ten p.m., not so late that we'd not be noticed – but the rest of me was on display.

'You're so wet,' he said.

Until that night I'd found it difficult to orgasm in public. Either I couldn't relax enough or there wasn't enough time to get me there. That night was different. Action Man got the idea of what I liked very quickly, so for once I wasn't distracted and barely noticed the footsteps and chatter of people retrieving cars near by. James sucked on my clit, and I felt myself dripping over his face. I rocked slowly back and forth, adjusting my position so my clit made direct contact with his tongue. Ten minutes later I screamed as I came. I looked up to see if anyone heard or witnessed the action. There was no one there.

I put my clothes back on, kissed James goodbye, then drove to the exit and dropped him off. The next day he went to Amsterdam and I went to work. I didn't know when I'd see him again, especially as I'd just learnt that seeing James would be a lot more complicated than he'd earlier indicated. When I asked him the exact nature of his relationship with his wife, he came clean. 'I have to be discreet.'

'So, you sleep together.'

'Not all the time.'

'Most of the time. Just not when you're on the road, maybe?'

'Something like that.'

I remained starry eyed at the thought of going out with someone with such an exotic job. And he really gave great oral. I was not in the market for a boyfriend then, but I am always in the market for getting what I want, when I want it. I can either wait around for Action Man to return, I thought, or I can go online or back to the personals and put myself out there again. If James and I got together again, great. Meanwhile, I went back to the personals.

Unavailable men, whether workaholic or married, are a waste of time. I end up frustrated or pissed off or wondering how many times I'll be stood up. I went back to the list of phone numbers I'd compiled after placing the *Independent* ad and called one of the contenders.

My next date was with Harry, a photographer who lived in Bristol. I spoke to him a few times on the phone and thought he sounded funny and sweet. In his response to my ad he'd said, 'I look like a cross between Bob Hoskins and a Kray brother. I'm looking for an uncomplicated woman who isn't completely psychotic like the last woman I dated. I like Americans girls, too. Call me.' He was coming to London the next Friday night, so we arranged to meet at Soho House. He promised to buy me martinis and make me laugh. 'You won't be disappointed,' he said on the phone. 'I really am a nice guy. And, just so you know, I'm not your typical wanky London photographer-type either.'

We arranged to meet at nine p.m. and he was late. Not a good sign. I wore my fishnets, high black stilettos, a navy-blue silk taffeta skirt and a sleeveless grey sweater. I draped a burgundy shrug over the top, something I had bought off eBay six months earlier for $11.99 and shipped to Frank, who then posted it to me. It was my favourite piece of clothing, because it was cool and original but didn't make me look like I was trying too hard.

Harry walked into the Circle Bar and immediately I recognised him from his description. He looked like something out of *Lock, Stock and Two Smoking Barrels* – kind of cute in that stocky East End-thug-type way, but with a friendly round face. He was about 5'9" and completely bald, with massive shoulders and an equally massive stomach. I don't do fat, my type being tall and emaciated; blond is a plus, too, and bald a definite minus. He may have been the nicest guy in the world, but I was not interested in a big bald man. But I decided to be polite. It was Friday night; he had come up from Bristol and I had nothing else to do. Plus, I figured the chance of running into someone frisky at the House while I was there was pretty high. I made small talk to fill the time.

Sitting next to me on the sofa, Harry told me he had a son, just out of school, and had come to London to chaperone his son to various interviews required in his applications to the fashion colleges. His son was a talented designer, Harry said, adding, 'Not gay, just in case you were wondering.'

I assured him I wasn't.

'Most people do,' he said. 'I know it's unusual for a boy to be interested in fashion and not be gay.' He told me he had visited St Martin's that day and had been very impressed. 'I'm hoping he goes there. It's a good school.'

'Yes, it is,' I agreed, 'and full of pretty girls, too.'

'Well, that's another bonus, of course,' he said, laughing. Harry moved closer to me, until his head was practically on my shoulder.

It was about an hour after we'd met and my interest in keeping up the conversation began to wane. Then I spotted Patrick, a sexy Irish poet in his late twenties, walk into the bar. I'd seen him at Soho House at least half a dozen times since joining the club two years earlier. Once he had tagged along with my girlfriends and me when we went dancing at Momo's, a Moroccan restaurant and club off Regent Street. I wasn't sure if he saw me but, as always, he was pretty hard to miss – about 6'4", with shoulder-length dark hair and a slim body perpetually encased in a single-breasted brown wool suit. He had dark-brown eyes that matched his suits, and a charming disarming smile. I'd had the hots for him ever since the night he recited one of his poems to me – called, appropriately enough, 'The Philanderer' – in the club's Drawing Room. Patrick was one of the few men on my mental list of guys I really wanted to fuck. He was a good ten years younger than me, but I'd seen pictures of him in *Tatler* with Lady this or Dame that, looking like an old-fashioned lady's walker, so I assumed he liked older women.

I didn't want him to escort me. I wanted him to fuck me.

Now, by some miracle, here he was, alone and obviously looking for someone to buy him a drink. He was always working the impoverished-poet act. I'd never seen him buy a drink for anyone, including himself. I was up for the opportunity to indulge his tradition.

So I made my excuses to Harry, telling him that I had to wake up early the next day for an appointment with my personal trainer, and walked him out the door. I kissed him on Shaftesbury Avenue, then walked around the block and back into the House.

Patrick was standing at the Circle Bar when I returned. I walked up to him. 'Haven't seen you here for a while, Patrick.

You don't fancy coming dancing with me, do you?' I told him I was thinking of heading over to Momo's.

'Thanks, but not tonight,' he said. 'I think I'm just going to stick around here.'

Plan B. 'Want to get a table in the Drawing Room then?'

'Sure.'

This was my first time alone with Patrick. I was excited at the possibility he might come home with me. 'So, what's new, handsome?' I asked.

Like so many artists in their twenties, he was happy to talk about his latest project. 'I'm working on my music. Trying to get some songs together.'

'Songs?' I said. 'I thought you were a poet.'

'I *am* a poet,' he protested, 'but I'm working on putting my poems to music.' He told me he'd met some record company people at Soho House and they'd promised they'd listen to anything he put on tape. It sounded suspiciously vague. In the two years I'd been going to Soho House, I'd met many record, film and television executives, most of whom bragged about what they did for a living and told me they could use a PR agency. They'd ask me to follow up, and I would, sometimes even writing up a promotions plan. I never got a job from any of them. It was all talk, I learnt, the bullshit that follows too much drink and coke. Patrick, darling, I thought, you have a lot to learn.

I asked him his age. He told me he was twenty-nine.

I thought twenty-nine seemed too old to be entering the music industry with the aim of being a rock star. Most have had botox and a stint in rehab by that age. But, as I looked across the table at Patrick, I thought twenty-nine was perfect for me. His Irish accent was fetching. He seemed refreshingly innocent and sweet – no brittle edges. He wasn't hugely interesting to talk to, though, so I leant across the table and kissed him. He did not refuse me. He was a lovely kisser, with a gentle probing tongue that made me feel quite heady. I tossed my hair sexily and let it tumble winningly on to the table.

'Excuse me, ma'am,' I heard someone say.

I paid no attention. Then I smelt something burning.

'Ma'am, I think your hair is on fire.'

I looked up and saw a waitress hovering over our table, looking quite alarmed. As did Patrick, who pulled well away. 'Suzanne, your hair is on fire!'

My hair had fallen not on to the table, but into the candle on the table. The odour was foul and soon permeated the room. I put my hand to my head and felt the burnt ends. I did not want to spoil the kissing, so made a joke of it. 'It'll grow back.' In truth, I was embarrassed and wondered just how much hair had been burnt off and whether my expensive new hairdo was ruined. Was it now an asymmetrical Bananarama do like I'd worn in my university days?

Patrick said, 'You sure you wouldn't like to go to the bathroom and inspect the damage?'

'No,' I said. 'I want to kiss you.' I had waited a long time to get Patrick alone. I touched his cheek with one hand while pulling out clumps of hair with the other.

By one-thirty a.m., almost four hours since I'd met Harry and three since I'd hooked up with Patrick, I wanted to go home. 'Do you fancy coming back to my place, Patrick?' I told him I had a bottle of vodka there and suggested a nightcap.

'Sounds good,' he said.

We walked back to the China Town Car Park and got into my car. Suddenly I could smell Patrick, and it wasn't cologne. It was a mixture of tobacco and sweat, and it was not appealing. The first thing I'm going to do when we get back, I thought, is get this guy into the shower.

Patrick carried on talking about his desire to be a rock star. He might make a better gigolo, I thought. Especially if he bathed more frequently. I wondered if perhaps he did turn tricks. He seemed to have no money – or at least no willingness to spend it (I had picked up our drinks) and those expensive suits had to come from somewhere.

I couldn't have been more wrong. We got back to my place and I suggested we take a shower together. He declined, saying he was all right, didn't need one, was tired. 'Could we just have that drink and go to sleep?'

That was what he meant, too – sleep. He explained he'd been on a three-day bender and was just coming down. Then, adding as an aside, perhaps as a hint, he said he'd had so much sex in the previous two years he was bored to death of it all and just wanted to sleep. I believed him. His beauty exuded the atmosphere of someone who had got everything, and everyone, he wanted – except, perhaps, a record deal. But now it just exuded exhaustion. I pointed to my bed.

As I watched Patrick sleep, my interest in him waned. He was too young and too fucked up, I decided. At least I finally got this one out of my system, I thought, as I rolled to my side of the bed.

Fortunately, I had a lunch date the following day to look forward to, with a guy off Nerve. When I got up the next morning, I made Patrick some eggs and bacon, and thanked him for the evening. 'It was fun, Patrick, but I've gotta shoot off,' I said. 'No doubt I'll see you at the House sometime.'

Patrick gave me a quick kiss on the lips and was off. I was part disappointed, part pissed off and one hundred per cent horny. I had counted on more than the bed-and-breakfast routine. If my Nerve date is half-decent and sexy, I thought, I'll suggest an afternoon delight.

The kids were with their father; I'd done the laundry and tidying up, and I was free. I hoped after lunch I'd be spending the afternoon in bed.

I met Ian at the Westbourne, a gastropub in Westbourne Park. It was very crowded with shoppers taking refuge after their pricey morning on the Portobello Road. I saw Ian walk in. He was my type: over six feet tall, blond, slim. His hair was messy, and he walked in a casual way that he probably thought was cool but that reminded me of guys who smoke too much pot and take too much E. His pace was so languid, so slow, that, even though he was almost a foot taller than me, he walked at half the pace. Everything about him was slow and relaxed.

We talked a little about our history. Somehow it wasn't a surprise when he said, 'I used to have a smack problem, a really bad smack problem.' He said all his friends had done the stuff. They were into the Happy Mondays and the Stone Roses.

'I had a friend in one of the bands,' he said. 'We used to hang around, get wasted. I was in a pretty bad way, then I just got lucky and through a friend got this great job.' He was a copywriter for a huge natural beauty-products company that had shops around the world. 'Now I write all the stuff you read on the bottles.'

Wow, that's some story, I thought, looking at him and trying to work out whether I really did want to fuck him. I also wondered if he'd really got off the smack or had just said that for my benefit. He was about thirty-three, so a bit young for me, but, after a couple glasses of wine and a satisfying baked trout, I was in a good mood and he was getting sexier and sweeter.

'Do you fancy a walk around Portobello, Ian?' I asked.

He said he did, so we walked towards the Westway and wandered around the market. I didn't plan on buying anything, but thought it would kill time while I decided what to do with him. I'm always conscious when shopping with men that most view it as punishment. Ian was well behaved, not in a rush, so he passed this impromptu test.'

'Care to come back to my house for a cup of tea?' I asked. He deserved a reward for good behaviour, plus it was tea-time now. I'd spent enough time in public spaces with this man and could just as easily serve him tea at home, in bed, as take him to a café.

'Tea? At yours? Do you have a car?'

We were back by four and in bed, with our teacups, by four-thirty. The sex was surprisingly good – languid and sensuous.

Ian had an unusual oral technique that was new to me and really turned me on – licking my pussy, pausing, and then licking again, building anticipation for more. It was a real departure from most men's technique, which tends to involve licking so hard it brings pain, or roughly thrusting their fingers up the vagina as if unaware there are sensitive nerves there. Then there are men whose mistake is to use continuous pressure; they end up with a numb tongue and a woman asking for more time and more variety and frustrated by his inability or unwillingness to provide either. Worse, in a sense, are those who spend so little time down below the gesture hardly counts as foreplay. Too many men treat the female organ like they do their own, unaware that, although theirs responds to the aggressive approach, the female requires a lighter touch. The clitoris has just as many nerve endings as the penis, but they're concentrated in an area a fraction of the size.

Ian's technique involved continuous movement and steady pressure. His tongue was very deliberate. He would start licking my pussy, then stop, start again, then stop. It was arousing because I never knew when he was going to start or stop, and so I hovered between pleasure and the expectation of more pleasure. He was incredibly intuitive, leaving me waiting for more, but not for too long, and therefore always satisfied. I'd never had anyone eat me like that. Clearly, to Ian, providing this service was not a duty. I sucked his cock for a while but, for a change, that Saturday afternoon the focus was on me. A half-hour later I came, without worrying about pleasing him at all. He was satisfied to jerk himself off . . . in my mouth.

Afterwards, we lay in bed a while, then took a shower together. Ian picked up the creams and lotions he saw on the shelf and quizzed me about them all. Did I actually like that stuff? Did I ever read the directions? He read the labels on my shower gel and conditioner, comparing his own copywriting with Vidal Sassoon's. Poor guy. Even after a good lay, he couldn't leave his job behind.

7. A VISIT TO THE CLINIC

A few weeks after I'd last seen him, I got a call from James, asking if I wanted to meet up for lunch that day. My Action Man had just come back from a couple of months in the Middle East. We'd been seeing each other whenever he happened to be in London, which was not very often.

'What did you have in mind?' I asked.

'Your place.' I had told my receptionist I'd be taking a long lunch.

At one p.m. he pulled up outside my house.

We went straight upstairs to my bedroom. Throwing off my clothes, I said, 'Good to see you.' I looked at his hard cock and then knelt down and put it in my mouth.

'Plenty of time for that later,' he said. 'You know how quickly I come. Sit on my face instead.'

He lay down on the bed and I squatted over him. Facing my headboard, I grinded on his mouth, until twenty minutes later I had my orgasm. I grabbed a rubber and slipped it on his still-hard cock. He took me from behind and as usual came in about two minutes.

'Do you fancy a tuna sandwich?' I said after, laughing. 'It doesn't feel right, you coming over for lunch and not getting any.'

I made the sandwiches and we sat down at the kitchen table. Then he told me his wife would be away for the weekend. 'If you're free on Saturday night, I can bring my camera over and take some pictures of you,' he said. 'I can stay the whole night.'

'A whole night?' I said archly. 'That calls for a celebration. Should I order a cake?'

'Why don't we go to a fetish club instead,' he suggested. 'I'd love to see you in rubber.'

During our many long-distance phone-sex sessions, I'd learnt that James was a voyeur. He fantasised about going to fetish clubs and, as a photographer, he liked the idea of taking hot photos of his play pals. Until he met me, most of his fantasies had gone unrealised. His wife wasn't interested. I figured that, since a whole night with James came along so rarely, I had to make the most of it. I suggested Torture Garden. It was a club I'd been to a couple of times before, with another guy I'd also met off the web. He looked dreadful in rubber – it takes a certain confidence and physique to carry it off, and he had neither – and I'd stopped seeing him shortly after that fiasco. James, I knew, would look hot in a pair of PVC chaps. And, knowing how much he liked to watch, I thought it would be fun to dress up and be photographed by him.

He got in his car to go back home, and I skipped up the road, all the way back to my office.

When James arrived on Saturday night, he pulled two suitcases out of the boot of his car. We went up to my bedroom and he unpacked tripods, lights, cameras and lenses, as if he were prepared to shoot Kate Moss for a *Vogue* cover and not just a few dirty snaps of me.

'How long's this going to take?' I asked. I knew he took his photography seriously, but we had lots to do that night.

'It's *your* photo shoot,' he said. 'What do you have in mind?'

I told him I wanted soft, erotic nudes that would show off my newly toned body. 'Something I wouldn't be too embarrassed to hang on the walls one day, after my kids move out.'

I took off all my clothes and posed on my bed naked, occasionally masturbating. Having a camera aimed at me brought out my exhibitionist tendencies. I found the whole thing a big turn-on.

'How would you like me to pay for this?' I asked after an hour.

In reply he put down his camera, approached the bed and buried his head between my legs. Afterwards, he said, 'I think we're even.'

We went to Torture Garden a little later, and I got fucked a million different ways in the Couples Room. James thought all his Christmases had come at once.

The next morning over breakfast, he said, 'So. What have you been up to since I last saw you? Have you been a busy girl?'

'I haven't been sitting at home twiddling my thumbs, if that's what you're implying.' I told him about an architect named Keith I'd fucked, who'd wanted to tie me up; he was studying Japanese rope bondage and wanted the practice. And I mentioned a graphic designer named Graham I'd arranged to meet in the health club at One Aldwych, where I'd given him a blowjob in the hotel's quiet steam room.

Sounding concerned, James asked if I'd ever been checked for STDs. 'I know you use condoms, but there's always a slight risk of catching something. It might be a good idea to get checked out, considering how sexually active you are.'

I wasn't offended. I thought he was probably right, that it wasn't such a bad idea. And then I thought, I wonder if he knows something I don't. I hadn't been tested for an STD since my early twenties, after I'd gone out with an Italian hairdresser who, three weeks after our last date, phoned me up to say,

'Suzannahhh, I'm so sorry to tell you, my darling, but I have the gonorrhoea.'

'Have I given you anything?' I asked James. 'When was the last time you got tested?'

'Me? About six weeks ago. I'm clean,' he said. 'It's just that, since we last met, you told me you've been fucking around.' He was stating the obvious. 'I don't want you to take it the wrong way.'

Suddenly feeling paranoid, the next morning I made a few phone calls and learnt the only nearby walk-in clinic was St Mary's, in Paddington, a large NHS hospital off the Edgware Road. I'd given birth to my younger son there and remembered it as a gloomy place with faded yellowish walls and stale hospital-smell air.

I phoned my receptionist to tell her I had a doctor's appointment, dropped my kids off at school and then drove to the hospital. I arrived at nine a.m. and already the waiting room was completely full, with a crowd representing the full range of humanity. I saw university students, obvious prostitutes, Eastern European immigrants and a few post-menopausal women who looked like they may have wandered into the wrong part of the hospital. What united us was our nervousness and displeasure at being found out.

'Know you're gay and feel alone?' asked one poster on the wall. 'Come to the teenage gay group this Wednesday.' Another advertised: 'Teenage STD Clinic Walk-in Every Tuesday 10a.m.–1p.m.' The brochures in racks each spotlighted a different disease – chlamydia, herpes, hepatitis C, AIDS, gonorrhoea, syphilis. Graphic designers must be making a bomb producing so many STD brochures for the NHS, I thought.

I sat on an uncomfortable plastic chair shaped like a bucket. I was wearing a black-and-white pinstripe Paul Smith skirt, Baldinini high heels and a pink fitted Thomas Pink blouse. I was overdressed for the occasion. If I'd known what a shithole this place was going to be, I'd have worn my Juicy tracksuit, I thought.

I waited six hours.

The first thing doctors do at these clinics, not surprisingly, is ask about your sexual history. 'When was the last time you had sex?' asked the doctor, an attractive man in his late thirties.

I told him about the two guys the weekend before, then answered a series of questions about what we'd done together. Oral sex? Tick. Intercourse? Tick. Anal sex? Tick. Did I use condoms? Tick.

'Regular partners?'

'No.'

'And previous to that?' he asked.

I told him about the two guys the weekend before.

'Regular partners?'

'No.'

Oral sex? Tick. Intercourse? Tick. Anal sex? Tick. Condoms? Tick.

Then he asked me about the weekend before that, and received the same answers.

'Are you working?' he asked me.

'Yeah.'

He asked how many men I'd been with in the past two months. I gave a guestimate.

'Well, in that case,' he said, 'we can put you on the Fast Track programme.' I'd be assigned my own doctor, he explained, promising I'd be seen quickly when I came in for my regular visits.

'That sounds great,' I told him. I wouldn't have to wait six hours for check-ups with the merely promiscuous ordinary people.

'I'll just need you to fill in a few forms,' he said as he began to draw my blood. 'How many customers do you have in an average week?'

Suddenly, I figured out what was going on. 'When you said, "Am I working?" you meant "working girl", didn't you?'

'Yes.'

'Oh. I thought you meant, "Do you have a job?"'

'No,' he said flatly.

'Oh, in that case, I'm not working. Well, I mean I *am* working,' I explained. 'I run a PR agency, but I'm not *working*, if you know what I mean.'

'Yes.'

'Does that mean I'm not eligible for the Fast Track programme?'

'No,' he said, shaking his head. 'I'm sorry, you're not.'

Driving home – by now, the workday was shot – I thought, Maybe there is something to be said for a steady partner after all. The novelty of fucking around was wearing off. I went through the inventory of men I'd slept with in the six months since my divorce. Most, I concluded, I didn't fancy enough to pursue anything steady. Those I did like and who appeared to like me, such as Action Man, weren't available. I was growing tired of negotiating meets with guys who lived south of the river. None of the websites I used let me search by neighbourhood and, since I lived north, I had to factor in the distance to a man as much as the attributes of the man himself, since just getting from one end of London to another can take two hours in bad traffic. What I really needed was a nice local boyfriend – nothing too serious but someone regular and fun.

I still had contenders left over from my newspaper ads, their phone numbers carefully typed on a piece of plain white paper now pinned to my kitchen bulletin board. Though I'd written cryptic notes beside the names, I no longer knew one from the other. 'Greg, tax lawyer, Australian, 6', slim, Earl's Court.' It wasn't a lot to go on. I devised a plan.

I needed to tweak my personal ad to indicate I was up for something steady, not just one fun night. And I needed to cast a wider net. Since I'd met or fucked most of the London-based guys on Nerve who were about my age, I didn't hold out much hope there. I decided to do a blitz campaign, and posted personals in *Time Out,* the *Evening Standard,* the *Guardian* and the *Independent*, as well as DatingDirect.com and

Match.com. The ads were free so I figured I had nothing to lose.

Sexy, smart, funny, fit, London-based American media chick, 41, seeks handsome, successful, funny, fit guy for regular weekend date.

Within a couple of weeks I had more than a hundred replies, and the culling began: John, the East End cabbie who had flexible working hours but lived with his mother; Max, the American banker, who couldn't see me on weekends because he had a wife but might be able to sneak out of the house every once in a while for some 'fun'; Patrick, the lighting designer, who had an open relationship with his wife and who left a long message telling me how he enjoyed hearing her fuck other men while he sat in the kitchen reading the Sunday papers; Chris, a cameraman from Lancashire who didn't mind travelling. I felt like I'd posted a job ad in the *Guardian*'s Media section. If only I had a human resources manager who could sift through all the applicants, I thought. Trawling through the replies, listening to the messages, writing down the phone numbers, annotating the bios – it was a laborious task.

I looked at the growing list of names and didn't know where to begin. Should I sort them alphabetically and work my way from Aaron to Zahid, or go by location, job, hobby? I thought back to my late twenties, to when I got married. Back then, David would have been the only name on the list. How times had changed.

Would a carpenter make a better lover than a banker? I wondered. Should I get to know the tax-avoidance lawyer? He might come in handy. One respondent said he worked in the City. I'd never been out with a man who worked in the City before; in fact, I'd never been out with a man who was loaded. That, I thought, would be a novelty. Then, I told myself, You're a media chick. Think outside the box. That's when I hit on the idea of sorting the list by generation.

Confounded by so many possibilities, I contemplated how each age group had its own advantages. Younger guys could keep it up all night, but lacked the intellect and experience of an older man. Older men came with baggage, usually ex-wives and children and, consequently, debt. In between were guys in their thirties, many of whom were headhunting a wife or devoted to climbing the career ladder. I'd competed with a job before, and lost.

I decided to fuck one guy from each generation – twenties, thirties and forties. I drew the line at fifty – wrinkles and spare tyres don't appeal; I'll deal with them when I get there myself. I'd date one from each group for three nights in a row and, using that as my yardstick for future dates, decide which gener-ation to target.

My first choice was Tom, a thirty-two-year-old web geek off Nerve, chosen because he (a) lived a half-mile from my house and (b) had a passion for expensive classic racing cars. I thought he sounded cool. His picture showed a slim angular guy with cropped bleach-blond hair and pale skin. We arranged to meet in Queen's Park at a pub midway between the two of us.

He looked like his picture, only smaller. He wasn't much taller than me, and had the kind of pale skin that comes from spending too much time indoors at the computer, like Frank had. I was not exactly turned off by him, but neither was I turned on. After two drinks however, I was feeling frisky and thinking he looked a lot better than before and I began to fancy sucking his cock.

'So,' he asked, 'you want to come back and see my place? It's not very big.'

Your cock or your place? I wondered. 'Sure, let's go.'

Tom lived three minutes down the road in a small cramped room in a flat that he shared with another guy. His bedroom consisted of a double bed and all the contents of an electronics store – mixing boards, turntables, computer monitors, plus wires everywhere. It was a mess and I don't do mess. Then I saw a bulge in his pants and thought, Well, I can do mess for one night.

We fumbled around on the bed for a while. He had a good-sized cock and knew what to do with it, and he could use his tongue as well. He went down on me for about twenty minutes and I sucked his cock, and, for a change, here was a man who didn't come in five minutes. Then I put a condom on him and fucked him, me on top, until I came. Afterwards I sucked him off. He came in my mouth. Like most of the guys off Nerve, he enjoyed sex and was good at it.

Geeky guys are like fat girls – they are so happy to actually be getting any, they learn early on how to please a partner and spend a lifetime devoted to doing so. I should know. I had once been one of those fat girls – with pimples. With geeky guys, if you get past the conversations about hard drives and RAM, you're in – and they're in you. I got the feeling Tom would have gone down on me or fucked me all night if I'd wanted him to. He wasn't selfish. This is why my friend Emily only dates web geeks.

We lay together after coming, snuggling on his messed-up bed. I left at midnight, about four hours after we'd met at the pub, explaining I had work the next day and didn't want to be tired. 'That was fun,' I said.

He gave me a lingering kiss. 'I had a good time too,' he said. 'I'll try and give you a ring later in the week.'

I kept Mr Thursday Night's number, because he was local and I thought, In a weak moment, I might want to get laid. He never called.

Mr Friday Night turned out different to how I had planned. I'd anticipated a date with a handsome, sophisticated middle-aged Frenchman I'd met in the real world a few weeks earlier. I'd gone out to celebrate my girlfriend Michelle's forty-fifth birthday. We were at the Light Bar in the St Martin's Hotel, a long, narrow dark room that's members only, but Michelle knew someone at the door and had arranged to take us there as a special treat. We were drinking mojitos and talking, as we usually did, about men.

'You really should get yourself a real boyfriend, Suzanne,' she said. 'All this fucking around isn't good. You'll get a bad reputation. People will talk.' Her tone was so judgemental.

'What people?' I asked.

She offered no specifics.

'Anyway, I'm having fun. I'll find a boyfriend when I want to find a boyfriend.' That's when I noticed a handsome guy sitting next to me on the banquette. I could tell he was eaves-dropping, or maybe hearing the words 'fucking around' perked his ears.

'So, you like casual sex?' he said with a strong French accent.

'From time to time,' I said. 'With the right person.'

Michelle glared at me.

He introduced himself as Philippe and asked if I'd ever been to a Paris swinging club. I told him I had not. I looked at him more closely. He was the proverbial tall, dark and handsome man. The tea lights on the table caught the grey flecks in his jet-black hair. He told me he'd just turned forty.

'You're looking pretty good for forty,' I said, and I meant it.

'It helps not drinking and smoking,' he said. 'My vice is women.'

I was intrigued.

'I love women,' he added. 'Young women.'

Oh, well, I thought, I'm out. 'So, these young women,' I said, 'where do you meet them?'

He mentioned a couple of bars I never went to because they were full of skinny young model-types on the lookout for sugar daddies. I knew where I didn't stand a chance. 'We could meet up sometime, if you'd like.'

'I thought you didn't like older women,' I said.

'I think we could have some fun.'

'So do I,' I said, and gave him my number.

'This is supposed to be *my* birthday party, not yours,' said Michelle.

I thought she was joking but she was not joking at all.

My French gigolo rang me up the day after we met and we arranged to 'have some fun' for that weekend. A few days later, he was ringing my front door; we kissed and went straight to my bedroom. No hanging out, no chit-chat. He was focused. He just wanted to lick my pussy for a half-hour until I came. So I let him. He kept his boxer shorts on, but his hard-on was evident. I asked if I could suck his cock.

'Another time,' he said. 'A woman like you, she gets bored easily. I want to save something. I will give you a little bit at a time. Then you will want to see me again.'

He'd misjudged me. I enjoy my starter, main course and dessert all served at the same time. Still, he looked like a movie star and made me come without demanding any satisfaction of his own. Guys like that deserve a second date.

We arranged to meet the following Friday night at Soho House. As I drove to our rendezvous, I wondered what he had in mind for the next course. The previous night, I'd been with Tom, the web geek. I wondered how Mr Friday Night would compare.

He was already in the Circle Bar when I arrived, drinking a mineral water. I was wearing a short Burberry kilt, a black crop-top sweater and high Patrick Cox shoes. I ordered a vodka and orange and propped myself up against the bar.

Just then, Philippe's phone rang and he went out in the hallway to answer it. 'I'm really sorry, Suzanne,' he said when he came back. 'I've got bad news. My girlfriend, she is at my apartment.' He explained that she'd lost her keys and would be staying at his flat for the night. And now she wanted to know when he was coming back.

'That really fucks things up, doesn't it?' I said.

'I'm really sorry,' he said. 'I'll make it up to you.' He kissed me once on the left cheek and once on the right and left the bar.

This is why I don't go out with middle-aged guys, I thought. There's always someone in the background. I made a mental note to scratch anyone in their forties off my list.

It was now eleven p.m. I looked around the bar and spotted Lance, the magazine editor I'd fucked a couple of months earlier, who had the ratty apartment and bad taste in bedding.

I didn't want to go home alone. 'Hi, Lance. What are you doing later on?'

'Tonight?'

'Yes, tonight.'

'I'm going to visit my grandmother early in the morning, Suzanne. You can't come home with me tonight.'

'The woman who gave you the duvet cover?' He didn't know what I was talking about and I didn't explain. 'OK. Bye,' I said, and walked to the other side of the bar towards another familiar face.

He was wearing a pair of natural linen trousers with a drawstring waist, a white Katherine Hamnett linen shirt, untucked, and a loose brown suede blazer. He reminded me of Johnny Depp, or a forty-two-year-old three-stone-heavier version of Johnny Depp. His name was Daniel and I'd seen him at Soho House many times before. He was a piece of their furniture. I'd never been there when he wasn't.

I'd met him twice before. The first time, I was standing at the bar with beautiful stinky Patrick, who was nagging his friend for neglecting his girlfriend. The friend turned out to be Daniel.

Our second introduction didn't leave a great impression either. I was sitting at the bar with my friend Gill, the editor of a women's magazine and Daniel was standing on my other side. Gill and I weren't close friends, but we had a lot in common. Our children had at one time attended the same local nursery, and her ex-husband was an old acquaintance from my days running nightclubs in the mid-80s. We were both feisty media chicks in our mid-forties, both single mums, and that night was a long-overdue girls' night out to catch up, have a bitch and get drunk. Except the bar was fairly full and both of us kept running into people we knew or who knew us. So our little group of two soon became two more with Gill talking to an old boyfriend she hadn't seen for ages, and me getting roped into a corner with Daniel.

'Would you like to read the first paragraph of my novel?' he said. 'It's the best first paragraph ever written.' He then produced about two hundred pages of loose paper from what looked like a record bag, and dumped it on the Circle Bar, not waiting for a reply. He had a worn-in face and the air of someone who'd slept in his clothes once too often and didn't mind. I couldn't decide whether he was bohemian or alcoholic, or both.

What kind of novelist carried their novel in a bag? Gill and I suspended our conversation and listened as he read the first paragraph aloud.

Jesus got nailed when he was about my age. He should have used a better lawyer than his dad. Big mistake, that. The old man didn't even turn up at court. Better things to do.

He was right – not a bad start. But that night I wasn't in the mood to make any new friends or to talk to a virtual stranger about his prose. Besides, this stranger looked drunk. His eyes were yellowish and cloudy. Plus, his pick-up line exuded an unsettling combination of arrogance and desperation, a real turn-off.

'You're right,' I said, 'not a bad paragraph.' I turned my back.

Gill was giving me a look that said, 'Watch out, he could be a nutter.' She hadn't even engaged him.

Daniel quickly changed tack and said, 'Nice ass.'

Yeah, well, I thought, after six and half thousand lunges and three years' work with a personal trainer, it better be nice. 'Thank you,' I said, and turned my back again. He left the room. That was meeting number two.

I hoped third time lucky.

I'd struck out twice already, with Philippe and Lance. The clock was creeping past midnight, and, standing with his back against the wall facing the Circle Bar, Daniel looked OK. I knew the likelihood of his rejecting me (or anyone else) was zilch, and I just wanted an easy in-and-out.

'Do you want to fuck me?' I said.

I pushed him into the wall and gave him a deep hard kiss. His mouth tasted like Stella Artois and Hamlet cigars.

'Of course,' he said, and lifted up my skirt for everyone to see, saying, in a loud baritone, 'Look at the great ass I'm taking home tonight!'

We took a cab home to mine, because he was unemployed, and was living with his parents in Somerset now. If I hadn't asked him to come back to mine, it would have been some other girl.

We got back to my place at about three a.m. and immediately he plopped a line of coke on my coffee table. I didn't do the stuff, but watched as he snorted it. I took all my clothes off and sat on the sofa, waiting for him to finish with his coke so he could concentrate on me. I lay down on the sofa, my head on one of the armrests and my legs spread apart, and looked at him. He couldn't get a hard-on. He was back hovering over the coke. Then he lifted his nose from the table and dived straight into my pussy, every once in a while lifting his head to tell me about this great novel he was trying to get published. I really wanted to get fucked but I could see that wasn't going to happen, not with a coke dick, but he really loved giving oral, I discovered. I think he must have eaten my pussy for about two hours, until I said, 'It's OK, you can stop now.' At least he does oral sex, I thought, and this hasn't been a complete waste of time.

'Have you heard about the Sick Million Dollar Man?' Daniel asked. 'He would get up and save the planet or whatever, but he's got a really bad cold. He can hardly get out of bed. Flu. It could be contagious.'

He had taken so much coke we both stayed up till seven-thirty in the morning. He'd been talking and eating my pussy on and off since midnight. I realised I liked him. He made me laugh. Despite being tired and a little pissed off that I hadn't got properly fucked, I hadn't felt so comfortable with anyone for a long time.

I kicked him out of bed at two-thirty that afternoon and went to meet some friends for lunch at a gastropub in Notting

Hill. I gave Daniel a lift back to the station. 'I'll call you in the middle of the week sometime,' he said.

'That's OK,' I responded. 'I'm really not that kind of girl. Don't feel you have to say that shit.'

He smiled and I drove off.

That evening, I was back to my experiment, this time sampling the twenties generation. A twenty-three-year-old wannabe writer named Nick had left a message in my *Time Out* voicebox. I told him to meet me at Soho House at eight. I walked in wondering what the staff must have thought, having seen me, and my ass, the night before with Daniel, and now, not twenty-four hours later, with a man almost young enough to be my son.

Nick was a tall, hunky Australian surfer type, with a mop of ash-blond hair. We'd communicated mostly by text message since first making contact, the preferred communication method for the twenty-something generation, I discovered. He always managed to say a lot in sixty characters.

ARE YOU AS HOT IN REAL LIFE AS YOU SOUND IN TIME OUT? (fifty-three characters.)

HOTTER. MUCH HOTTER. WHY DON'T YOU MEET ME AND FIND OUT? (fifty-six characters.)

I'M PRETTY BUSY AT THE MOMENT. LET ME GET BACK TO YOU. (fifty-five characters.)

It sounded like a classic chicken-out. But a week later he sent another text.

YOU STILL FREE TO MEET UP?

SURE. I tapped into my phone, and now here I was back at Soho House.

We sat at a small table in the Drawing Room – the same room where I'd burnt my hair a few months previously while staring into Patrick's pretty blue eyes. There might have been only five years' difference between these two men, but that was where the similarities ended. Whereas Patrick had been all smooth moves, a modern-day gigolo, Nick was all nerves, constantly glancing around the room as if he thought he might be asked for his ID or told to leave. He was thrilled to find himself in such a grown-up exclusive club.

We didn't have much to say to each other, but he was nice to look at and, as I contemplated my generation-sampling experiment, I thought, Well, that's the point of going out with younger boys; they're nice to look at.

I let him do most of the talking. He said he was designing websites for an internet company, just filling in time before his Kerouac-style novel was published. He had an agent but so far no publishers.

The bar was dead. Saturday nights always are at Soho House, so after a couple of drinks I suggested we go to my place. I wanted to check out the merch.

I hadn't been with a twenty-three-year-old since I was about twenty-three myself, and now, almost twenty years later, I knew why. It was straight to the main event. No warm-up act. No style. No finesse. No foreplay, no kissing, no nothing, except straightforward missionary-style pounding. His only advantage over men twenty years his senior was that, after he popped, he got hard again. Mr Saturday Night was in the door at midnight and out the door by one. He wanted the old in-and-out, and he got it.

By Monday morning, I'd weighed up the pros and cons of Messrs Thursday, Friday and Saturday Nights and came to the conclusion that, although none of them was perfect, I should stick to men my own age. At least they can hold a conversation, and they have had enough relationships to know what they want in a girlfriend and in bed. From a financial point of view, I thought that, if they hadn't got screwed over by their first divorce, they would be more financially stable. I didn't need a millionaire, just someone who could afford to take a weekend break in Prague and spring for the occasional exotic holiday. Or at least not expect me always to be the one having to pay for the fish and chips and Taittinger. Now all I had to do was find one of these guys. Nagging in the back of my mind was the hope that I would hear from Daniel again.

8. THE LIVE-IN

On Wednesday evening, the phone rang. 'Have you found my mobile?' It was Daniel.

'No.'

'Sure one of your kids hasn't hidden it or something?'

'It's not here, Daniel. Is that the only reason you've rung?'

'Mmmn', I heard on the other end.

'Didn't you want to tell me how much you enjoyed being with me on Friday night,' I continued, 'and that you've realised it was love at first sight?'

'Mmmn. Well, maybe. I could be thinking that too. What about you?'

'I'm thinking, if you weren't such an alcoholic cokehead, you'd be just perfect.' We'd had just one fuck, the weekend before, but already I was on to him.

A week later, I'm meeting his parents. And he's meeting mine. And my kids.

I knew he'd passed the test when my elder son, Alfred, told him, 'You know, my mum has a lot of boyfriends. And, when she farts, it smells really bad.'

'Yes, I know,' Daniel agreed, presumably to both statements.

'And a year from now, you won't be around.'

'That's OK,' said Daniel, 'because even if I'm not, I know where you live and I can track you down.'

The first few weekends visiting him at his parents in the country were great, until the novelty of getting out of London wore off. I've never really been much of a country girl. I don't really care about trees, fresh air, birds. The only aspect of the country that appeals to me is curling up under a down duvet, in the dead of winter, with a log fire burning, a glass of brandy by the bedside and someone else cooking dinner.

I resisted his moving in as long as possible. I didn't want a live-in boyfriend, having just seen my husband off just over six months earlier. And I knew he was still doing coke because often, after spending the night with his friends (he sometimes stayed with them, saying he didn't want to overstay his welcome at my place) he'd tell me he hadn't slept at all. I knew what that meant, just as I knew where the constant talk, talk, and more talk came from. Coke chat has always done my head in.

After eight weeks, I thought, Fuck it, he might as well move in. It was not so much because I wanted him to, but because I couldn't stand the commute to his parents' house.

I was playing angel more than girlfriend. As with David, whom I'd saved from the dole, and Frank, whom I'd hoped to rescue from his dreary life and negative outlook, I had now, in Daniel, another puppy to rescue. He was homeless. He had a coke problem. And a drink problem. And he hadn't worked in months. A four-star disaster. I told him he could move in – just for a while, I said, until he sorted out his career and his life. It wasn't so much about getting regular sex, although that was a nice side benefit, but because I thought I could help get him back on his feet.

I've never felt fully validated unless I'm needed. Frank had been the first person to recognise this need in me. One day, after I'd researched ways he could find work in London, he told me I didn't have to do everything for him, that he could look the laws up for himself, that it was enough just having me there for him. 'Be selfish, Suzanne. Do what *you* want to do,' he said. 'You take care of you.'

It had come as a revelation. I always thought the word 'selfish' was derogatory. Thinking back on my life, I saw the pattern. Step one: Find a guy who has a few problems. Step two: Love him and make him feel really secure. Step three: Watch him get back on his feet at the same time as I lose all sense of self and end up miserable. Frank hadn't meant his admonishment in a bad way. He had meant that I should stop thinking of others all the time and stop being a control freak. Just acknowledging I was one was a start.

So I had acknowledged it, and here I was starting the process all over again, this time with Daniel. Nobody's perfect. I had taken on the world-class challenge of trying to turn around his entire life. Perhaps I should have gone into nursing instead of PR.

One of the rules we negotiated early on in our relationship was that we both could carry on fucking other people as long as we were in the same room together. All of my gay male friends had told me that, when they entered relationships, one of the first things they did was set the sexual ground rules, recognising that monogamy wasn't a realistic option. That in mind, I explained to Daniel that, although I really liked him and the sex was good, I wasn't quite ready to give up fucking around.

'I don't want to settle down so soon, Daniel,' I said. 'I've got a good two or three years of fun left in me.'

He said he understood. 'As long as we're in the same room, that's fine,' he said. 'Because I don't trust you.'

It wasn't an ideal situation; I'd have preferred to be off on my own. But I thought it a reasonable compromise, and I recognised why he wouldn't want me going behind his back for sex – there was always the possibility I might fall in love with someone else. Six weeks into our relationship we were standing in my kitchen when I blurted out, 'I love you.'

'I love *you*, Suzanne,' said Daniel. And I knew he meant it.

Daniel had participated in plenty of threesomes over the years. He was a seasoned player. So his acquiescing to my request for a semi-open relationship wasn't solely altruistic. We had our first swinging episode soon after our conversation. It was with Baz, a Dutch doctor Daniel knew from Soho House. They'd had threesomes before. The three of us were talking when Daniel turned to me and asked, 'What do you think of Baz?'

'He's handsome,' I said.

'Do you want to fuck him?'

'Sure.'

Daniel turned to Baz and said, 'Would you fancy coming back to ours and fucking my girlfriend?'

We walked into my front room and the three of us sat down on the sofa, me in the middle. I was wearing a leopard-print wraparound dress, no knickers, and a pair of black high heels. Daniel always insisted I wear no knickers. 'What women never understand,' he said, 'is that the biggest turn-on for men isn't skimpy panties but no knickers at all.' Ever since he'd told me that, I never wore knickers under dresses or skirts.

I put my legs on the coffee table in front of the sofa. Baz and Daniel each did a line of coke. Then I spread my legs just enough to expose my pussy.

'Isn't she absolutely fantastic?' said Daniel.

Pulling out his cock, Baz said, 'Yes. She is ... wonderful.'

'And she gives the best blowjob you'll ever have,' Daniel predicted.

I was already sucking Baz's cock, while Daniel was wanking off watching.

'This feels fantastic,' said Baz.

It was fun enough for me. Baz was tall and blond and good-looking and well hung, my type in every way except that he was humourless. He didn't get my New York wise-ass humour. But I didn't give a shit. I wasn't auditioning prospective boyfriends. All I wanted that night was a cock in my pussy and another in my mouth, and that's exactly what I got. We went up to my bedroom to continue the fun until about three in the morning, when Daniel said to Baz, 'I think you better go now,' just as the three of us were falling asleep together.

I looked at Daniel as if to say, 'What's all this about?' but Baz was already getting dressed.

'Too intimate,' said Daniel, with Baz within earshot.

The next morning our evening was Daniel's sole topic of conversation, even though in my head I'd already moved on. It wasn't memorable enough to dwell on.

That's the way it always is with me. Adult fun is just that. Though it's more interesting than bowling with friends or having a good barbecue, I don't attach the same value to sex that other women seem to. Sex is just another way to pass the time.

Perhaps this is a consequence of having been around the block a few times. When girls are younger, we all think every man who fucks us is a potential husband. It took me a long time to figure out that most of them just want to get laid – and nothing more. Now I feel the same way they do.

While Daniel was talking about Baz, I was reminded of a conversation I once had with a part-time sex worker at a friend's party. She said the only way she could do her job was if she forgot about her customers as soon as they walked out the door. She was always amazed when one would ring her up months later and say, 'Hello, how are you?' without saying their name first. She couldn't believe any of them would think themselves *that* memorable.

Daniel said, 'Wow, that was some night. Baz is pretty handsome, isn't he?'

'Yes, he's handsome enough. If a bit boring.'

'But you liked him, didn't you?'

'Liked him? Yeah, I liked him. He seemed like a nice guy.'

'And he has a nice cock. Does it feel nicer than mine?'

I began to suspect this was not the normal morning-after chit-chat. 'Look, what's with you? He's a nice boring Dutch doctor with a decent-sized cock. End of story.' I wasn't planning on dissecting the previous night. 'Are you jealous?'

Then Daniel said something that took me by surprise. 'I like the jealousy,' he said.

'You're weird,' I said and made breakfast.

What a complex man he was. He had had early success as a TV and print journalist, until one day he got sick of it, packed it all in and moved to Spain to write a novel no one wanted to publish. When he returned to London, he had been all but forgotten. New blood had come in; the internet had taken over, and no one wanted a drunken cokehead who scoffed at the net and refused to learn even how to send email.

In just a couple of years the whole industry had changed, and he had not. Daniel was a journalist from a different era. He had specialised in financial journalism, and claimed that in the pre-internet days journalists got half their stories from hanging out in the City pubs and talking to the traders over their lunch hour. 'Everyone who was a City journalist in the eighties has liver damage,' he told me. He made it sound as common as owning a Ford Fiesta.

Writers can put a story on the page, a skill that doesn't always transfer orally. Daniel, however, was a fantastic storyteller and had a reputation as Soho House's resident raconteur. He told me more than once about the time he and Rufus Sewell sat in the Drawing Room at the House one miserable December evening when, all of a sudden, a booming Welsh voice said, 'Is there anyone serving around here?' They turned and saw Tom Jones, alone, waiting for a drink. They asked him to join their table and by the end of the evening Rufus was at the piano accompanying Tom as he belted out the Welsh national anthem and some of his own songs, while Daniel sat watching. I was never sure whether to believe Daniel, if only because I'd never seen anyone play the piano at the House. But Daniel swore it was true and made it sound magical, even if it was a complete load of shit.

And he was sexy. He looked like an old-fashioned musketeer with his gaucho moustache and shoulder-length wavy brown hair. He had massive shoulders and a huge stomach that somehow he carried off. He was my Renaissance man: a good cook and a willing housecleaner, who enjoyed a bit of DIY, loved gardening and wanted to fuck me all the time. He used to fuck me over the kitchen table while the kids were upstairs playing with their GameBoys. Had Daniel been born about two hundred years earlier, he'd have been Lord Byron's sidekick. He was good with the kids, who liked him a lot, but he prefered to consider himself a man's man. There was absolutely nothing sissy about him. He was so heterosexual he wouldn't even let me touch his bum. 'Only gay men go up there,' he said, though he was happy to go up mine every day.

Together, we were the proverbial terrible twosome. I'd been honing my predatory skills in the months that followed my divorce, and now I had an accomplice. A typical Friday night consisted of going to Soho House, taking our place by the side of the Circle Bar, where it was impossible for anyone to walk by without having to squeeze past us. Typically that would lead to an introduction, and by the end òf the evening Daniel would say, 'Why don't you come home with me and my girlfriend for a threesome?'

Daniel must have had a reputation among the women there. They always came by to say hello to him, and I always wondered if this had something to do with Daniel's mastery of the oral technique. He had lost four of his bottom teeth (and never replaced them) from a marathon round of oral sex back in the early 90s.

'I'd been at the House and taken too much coke,' he told me. 'I was with a mate who worked for Saatchi's at the time. We met these two tall blonde birds and asked them if they wanted to go off with us to do some coke. We all went to the Saatchi offices and snuck into this boardroom with a fifty-foot-long table. I lay on the table licking coke off this girl's clit. She was grinding her cunt on my face for about three hours. I woke up the next morning and my teeth felt a bit funny and wobbly. They'd been loose from when I played rugby as a kid, but this was different. So I checked into the dentist and he pulled out a pair of pliers and yanked them all out. No anaesthetic, the bugger. They just came right out. But that was some night!'

Despite his public bravado, Daniel never kissed another woman after that night. He was too self-conscious of the missing teeth and never had enough money to get them replaced.

He was the only guy I'd had a relationship with who was utterly against type. He was not tall, not blond, not slim like the men I normally went for but, when we lay in bed together and he was wrapped around me, I felt protected by his big strong shoulders and arms. This was a novelty for me. I'd always been the fatter one in my previous relationships, and it was great not to worry about crushing someone if I rolled on to him in the middle of the night. My type was gentle and even slightly feminine. Daniel was a manly man in traditional ways – he drank beer, watched rugby and fell asleep in front of the television at eight p.m. And he snored.

Although I had my doubts about him being good relationship material, he had other strong points. He loved my children. He had always wanted to have kids of his own and, when he met mine, I gave him free rein to treat them like they were. He would pick them up from the school bus stop (when he remembered), take them to the pub to watch the rugby, throw a ball around with them in the back garden. The kids adored him but were a little frightened of him. Once, when my elder son told me to go to hell after I'd told him to do his homework, Daniel chased Alfred up the stairs, fist in the air. He would never have hit my children but, after that, just raising his hand was enough to keep them in line. It was nice to have a man around the house who took an interest in the kids and wanted to help me out, too, especially one who fixed dinner often enough that I didn't feel like a slave to the kitchen. Despite him being a cokehead, unemployed, a smoker, overweight and a bit of a fuck-up, I liked having him around and thought, Well, at least he's entertaining and cooks me dinner.

Still, though it bothered me he wasn't scoring a job, it bothered me more he wasn't writing at all. When he'd read the opening paragraph of his unpublished novel the second time we met, I'd thought, At least he has aspirations. In Somerset one weekend, his dad proudly produced a yellowing newspaper clipping of a column Daniel had written five years earlier for the *Sunday Business* newspaper. It struck me as somewhat sad that he didn't have anything more recent to show me. Daniel had obviously once been the family's golden boy. He carried around a little notebook in his back pocket on which he'd scribble ideas for feature stories, yet in all the time we were together I only saw him write two things: food shopping lists and notes to the bank manager explaining why he needed to increase his overdraft.

I thought maybe he was blocked. He seemed to invent any excuse to explain why he was not writing. 'All the newspaper editors are twenty-five years old now. What do they know?'

After six months together, it started to grate on me. If he was such a fantastic writer, such a brilliant man, why couldn't he just sit down and write? Given that his was the one career that didn't require expensive tools or an office, it seemed perfect for someone who had no money.

'Why aren't you writing?' I asked one night after coming back from work, knackered. 'You haven't had a single thing published since I've met you. What's the problem? All you need is paper and a pen.'

'It's not that, Suzanne,' he said. 'I'm too old to write for free any more. I'm not going to work on another manuscript and be rejected. If I'm not getting paid, I can't write.'

What we really needed to discuss was a strategy for mending the bridges he'd burnt, or finding something else for him to do. Through drinking, drugging and arrogance, he had made himself unemployable by most of the national newspapers.

So we fell into a pattern of Daniel having sex with me, barking occasionally at the boys and cooking dinner a few times a week for all of us. He never seemed to do much else. After dinner I would find him asleep in bed fully clothed or passed out on the sofa. Many weeks, our Friday-night plans were scuppered when I'd be unable to rouse him from his nap. After a few months of this I got tired of trying. Still, when Daniel wasn't sleeping, we had a lot of sex.

Initially, the frequency and quality of the sex was my panacea. Daniel was a pro – as, I learnt on a holiday, he should have been. We were lying on the beach in the Costa Brava, during a two-week holiday that I was paying for. We'd spent most of the morning fucking, first in the bedroom in his parents' holiday home, then outside in the courtyard, then on the living-room sofa. We were lying together under a couple of towels, as the weather had suddenly got cold, when I said, 'So, how many girls have you slept with? Fucking seems to be your raison d'être.'

'I don't know,' he said. 'Maybe a couple of thousand.'

'A couple of *thousand*?'

'Well, are you counting the group sex?'

'Yes, group sex counts, I said.'

'Well, let's see. I've been having sex since I was fourteen. And there was a period of four years in my mid-thirties where I probably had five different girls a week, so that's … what?'

'Fifty-two multiplied by five, multiplied by four.'

'What's that?'

'About a thousand.'

'OK,' Daniel continued. 'And then maybe half of that time there were two girls at once, or two the same day, not to mention the years leading up to my thirties. So, maybe two and a half thousand.'

'That's a lot of girls,' I said, suddenly feeling almost virginal.

And that, he said, was why straightforward fucking didn't interest him much any more. There was the occasional vaginal penetration, but only as a precursor to my taking it up the ass. Mainly cunnilingus was his thing. For a long time, that was fine with me, though I knew it was partly because he was lazy. All he had to do was lie there with his mouth open. But, after six months of doing the same old thing every day, I wanted variety. I actually wanted good old missionary, just a regular fucking fuck.

One morning, I lay in bed next to him, thinking, if he fucks me up the ass one more time, I'm going to scream. Then I did scream. 'Why won't you just fuck me?'

He turned one sleepy eye towards me. 'I was waiting for that,' he said. 'I just find it boring, that's all.'

'Well, I don't!'

Soon after, he was taking Viagra as a little boost to overcome the boredom of straightforward sexual intercourse and to keep his dick hard while he did it. He'd buy it off some dodgy dealer he'd met in a pub, come home and split a 100mg tablet in half. The effect of the 50mg lasted him two days. But he said he had no control over when and where he'd get hard. We'd be on our way to the supermarket and he'd say suddenly, 'I think we should go home now,' and point to the crotch of his trousers.

'We need food. Can't you do something about that?'

'I'm afraid it's out of my control, Suzanne.'

I'd have to turn the car around so we could fuck for a couple of hours. I'd think back to when I was a teenager and my girlfriends and I would talk about boys. My friend Debbie educated me. 'They can't control it, you know,' she explained. 'It can just get hard for no reason and, when it does, they have to come. Otherwise it really hurts.'

I had grown up believing I was actually doing boys a service by sucking their cock, sparing them hours of pain. Now, all these years later, it still hadn't occurred to me that perhaps Daniel *could* control his erection and just didn't want to.

The first six months of our relationship was our honeymoon period. I still believed Daniel was actively looking for work and that this period of poverty might be over soon. He was carrying his little notebook around, making notes and telling me he'd had meetings with editors. Though not bringing in an income, he seemed to be trying. He had quit taking coke and promised to cut down on the cigarettes and alcohol. Meanwhile, I woke up most mornings to sex; my boys liked having a big guy around, and I came home after work to see my kids sitting quietly at the kitchen table, doing their homework and eating a snack he'd prepared for them.

After a half-year together and about four months after he moved in with me, my children went to summer camp in Upstate New York, and Daniel and I had a month to ourselves. We hung out at Soho House two or three times a week and had a couple of dinner parties on nights we stayed in.

After one of our dinners, a film producer who was a longtime friend of Daniel's took me aside in my kitchen. 'I'm so glad he met you,' he said. 'He was a bit of a mess before, but you seem to have straightened him out. I've never seen him look so healthy. What's your secret?'

'I fuck him every day.'

As the film producer took a drag on his cigarette, I was reminded of the most serious crime among Daniel's many misdemeanors. His smoking drove me crazy.

I had quit when I was twenty-seven after David gave me an ultimatum: 'It's me or the cigarettes. You choose.' It didn't take much convincing to make me quit when I calculated that, by quitting smoking, I'd both keep the boyfriend and save enough each month to buy two pairs of shoes. Daniel, on the other hand, was deeply attached to his Hamlet cigars. He loved smoking and, despite my pleas that he quit, he wouldn't, promising only that he would not smoke in front of me.

On my forty-second birthday, Daniel said, 'You say I don't do any real work. Just wait till you see how I transform that postage stamp you call your garden.' He bought flowers from the nursery to spruce up the beds. He also picked up some turf and patched a spot that had been worn away by a son who wanted to be a goalkeeper when he grew up and who, despite daily practice, never learnt how to save a ball without dramatically falling over, in the same spot, when making a catch. My garden did look lovely when David was done, but my biggest present was still to come: he promised to quit smoking.

That night I took my children to my parents' house for dinner. Daniel said he was going to stay in, as he wasn't feeling well, but on the way home I spied him in the doorway of a bar on the high street, cigarette in hand. I honked the horn and waved, and he waved back, tossing the cigarette behind him.

That pushed every button in my brain. I stormed through the front door and, cursing Daniel, grabbed a suitcase from the loft and threw as many of his things as would fit into it. The kids cowered in their rooms. I dragged the suitcase into the boot of my car, drove back to the bar and dropped the suitcase at his feet.

'You promised to quit smoking for my birthday and you couldn't even do it this one day,' I said. 'That's it. I've had it. Here's your stuff. Now give me back my keys.'

He looked stunned as he reached into his jacket and handed me my keys. I turned around and drove home.

Two hours later, after giving me time to cool off, he was at my door. 'C'mon, Suz, open the door. I'm cold.'

'Fuck off,' I shouted through the window. 'This time I'm serious. Find somewhere else to stay tonight.'

'Listen, you haven't given me all my stuff,' he said, and asked me to fetch his black sweater and brown loafers. 'You can pass them through the door and then I'll go.'

I got the sweater and the loafers. When I opened the door, Daniel pushed his way in and ran straight through the house to the back garden. He started pulling up the new turf and the flowers and tossed them over the fence into my neighbour's garden.

'Get out of the house!' I shouted. 'I'm calling the police.' I heard the kids crying upstairs. 'Leave!' I said. 'I'm not joking.'

Daniel stayed in the garden, kicking things. I went to the phone, dialled 999 and screamed, 'A man's just broken into my house! Please send someone quickly!'

Within five minutes three police vans were in front of my house. They left soon after, with Daniel in the back of one of the vans. At least he has a place to stay tonight, I thought.

Replaying the scene in my head the next morning, I reconsidered the severity of his crime. A night in the cell seemed rather a large price to pay for smoking a cigarette.

Later that day I drove to Daniel's brother Trevor's flat to drop off the rest of Daniel's things and to suggest he tell Daniel to find somewhere else to stay.

'We've been waiting to see how long it would take you to catch on,' he said. 'He's a fuck-up.' Trevor told me all of Daniel's girlfriends eventually chucked him out. 'He's a great liar. He'll tell you he's quit drinking and then go out and get drunk behind your back,' he said. 'He had no intention of quitting smoking, Suzanne. He probably just thought that was what you wanted to hear. He won't quit any of this. He can't.'

A few days later, Daniel came round to the house and charmed his way back in. 'Wow, that was quite a performance,' he said.

Still angry, I tried remaining stern but laughed despite my efforts.

'You were really convincing,' he said. 'I've never seen you quite that angry before.'

'Well, you said you'd quit smoking. That was meant to be my present. Some fucking present.'

'I like smoking – what can I say?' he said. 'I apologise. I'm really sorry. Though I think it's you who should be apologising for sending me to jail.'

'I'm not apologising.'

'Look, can I come back? I'll really try. I'm sorry,' he said. 'I really love you. You may be the only woman I've ever really loved. I want to spend the rest of my life with you. Just give me a couple of months. I'll clean up my act. If things don't work out by then, I'll move out. I promise.'

'OK,' I said. 'You've got a couple of months.'

9. BACK TO RIO'S

Daniel moved back in, carrying the suitcase I'd thrown at him just a few days before. As he unpacked and began hanging his clothes in my wardrobe, I thought, Why don't I just tell him to go now, while his bags are still packed?_But I said nothing. Maybe it was guilt. For all his bluster, Daniel was helpless, and I had come to suspect that what he had confessed several times before – that he had nothing without me – was true. I felt guilty that I'd stopped feeling the same way about him. Maybe I figured it was better to have a man around for my kids – even one who was an unemployed alcoholic smoker – than no man at all. I'd got used to Daniel, even if I knew the situation was probably unworkable. And I'd put a timeframe on this new stage in our relationship, so figured I had my get-out clause. 'We'll give it two months,' I said. Meanwhile, I figured, I'd get laid.

We'd been together ten months at this point and he hadn't written anything besides a few press releases through one-off jobs I'd got him through contacts at work. Journalism was a dead end for him. I rewrote his CV, as I'd done for David ten years earlier when he was on the dole. David got a fabulous job soon after, and I hoped the same might happen for Daniel.

'But I don't know what else I'd do if I didn't write,' he protested. 'That's what I do. I'm a writer.'

I wanted to say, 'Yes, you write a fantastic shopping list.' Instead, I said, 'C'mon, don't be defeatist. There's plenty you can do.' The two-month window I'd given him stretched to six, during which I concocted so many career possibilities for him I contemplated starting my own job centre, ChangeYourCareer.com.

'How about Hack Ltd, a freelance-writing agency aimed at getting PR stories into the national press?' I suggested one day, ticking off items on my list. 'Or Charm School for Boys, a workshop for men on how to pick up women. You've certainly slept with enough women to be an authority. Or See-Through Windows. Everybody needs window cleaners and you're enough of a voyeur you might get some perks, in addition to the cash.'

He actually tried all three, and many more besides. He'd start each career enthusiastically, but within a month he'd dump off, complaining, 'It's just not going to work. There's no money in this.'

'Every business needs time to grow,' I said, sounding like a life coach and cringing at the clichés coming out of my mouth. 'You can't expect it to be an overnight success.'

He didn't have the patience or dedication to give anything a few more weeks. Then one day I came home from work and he said, 'I've got a great job! It's selling corporate video services and the commission rates are really high. If I play my cards right, I could be pulling in twelve grand the first month.'

I tried to be supportive, thinking maybe what he'd need was to find jobs on his own, without my intervention. The telesales job lasted three weeks. He was sacked for turning up late too many days in a row. And he'd been sick the first four days of the job. In fact, Daniel was ill a lot. He'd catch the flu and be laid up in bed for three weeks, not the usual few days, and he always seemed tired.

He was still smoking and his breath was rank. He had put on over a stone since we'd met. His stomach had gotten noticeably larger. He was a mess.

But he still had charm. One summer Saturday afternoon, we drove to a local bar for a couple of happy-hour cocktails. It was a gorgeous sunny day and I was wearing a short green minidress. I pulled my car into a tight space opposite the bar with ease, even though there was barely three inches between my car and the ones on either side. Some young Australian guys sitting at an outdoor table watched me park, and apparently didn't believe it was possible for a woman driver to squeeze into a space that small. They were whooping and shouting at me. 'Way to go, girl!'

As we passed them going into the bar, one of them said, 'Nice parking.'

'If you think that's nice,' said Daniel, 'you should see what's underneath the dress. No knickers.'

I looked at Daniel as if to say, 'Can't you let it go *ever*?'

The boys laughed and then invited us to join them. We spent the afternoon in their company, first drinking at the bar before moving on to the flat that belonged to one of them. Mark, one of the lads, invited Daniel to do some coke.

'Do you mind?' he said, looking at me. He had told me he'd quit half a year earlier.

'It's your choice,' I said. 'I'm going soon.' I was drunk and tired and bored at this point, and I didn't want to hang out with a bunch of Australian guys half my age, cute as they were, and they were now drunker than me and moving on to the harder stuff.

Daniel said to the best-looking guy, 'Do you want to fuck my girlfriend?'

'Are you serious?' asked the guy.

I didn't stick around to hear his answer and walked out to my car and drove home.

Daniel turned up around eleven, two or three hours later, alone. I was watching television and he joined me. We smoked a joint, then fooled around on the couch for a while. Around three a.m. his mobile phone rang. It was Mark.

I heard Daniel say, 'Sure, we're just watching television and smoking a joint. See you in a few minutes.'

The doorbell rang ten minutes later. The three of us sat on the sofa, smoking a joint. Then Mark pulled out his cock and, turning to Daniel, said, in his thick Australian accent, 'Do you mind if your missus sucks my cock?'

'What do you think you're here for?' he answered.

His cock must have been about eight inches long, flaccid. It was the biggest I'd ever seen. When I started sucking it, Daniel, sounding offended, said, 'Flippin' heck, that's some huge cock!'

'I know,' said Mark. 'Sometimes I just like to flip it over my shoulder.' He whipped it from side to side like it was a twelve-inch Cumberland sausage.

I laughed. He was cute and funny. And so well hung.

'Sometimes,' he continued, 'I accidentally hit people in the face with it.'

Daniel didn't laugh. While I sucked Mark's cock, Daniel watched Mark get bigger and fatter and harder. Daniel sat on the floor against the sofa. After a few minutes, while Mark tried to fuck me doggy style on the sofa, I looked at Daniel. He appeared to be asleep, but given that he'd spent a couple of hours with the boys taking coke, I knew that wasn't likely. I could tell he was upset. He only enjoyed threesomes if he could be in control, the big man. And he was always comparing himself to the other guys, something I learnt from our first threesome with boring Baz.

Mark couldn't stay hard and, when I asked, 'Is there a problem?' he said, 'Sorry, I took some E before. You know how it goes.'

I tried to keep him hard by sucking him off again. He said, 'You give a fantastic blowjob.'

'So I've been told,' I said, stealing a glance at Daniel. I caught his eye. He wasn't asleep.

When Mark left a couple of hours later, I was relieved. It got boring trying to keep him hard, although it felt out of this world when he was.

The next morning I said to Daniel, 'What happened to you? You spend the entire afternoon trying to get one of those guys to come back with us, and then, when it happens, you get all jealous and pretend you're asleep.'

'You looked like you were enjoying Circus Cock a bit too much. That kid could have been in a freak show.'

'I thought that was the point,' I said. 'He's just an Australian kid with a big cock.'

'Yes, a very big cock.'

'Look, Daniel,' I said, 'if you're going to pull men for me to fuck, then you have to accept the consequences. Sometimes one of them is going to have a bigger cock than yours.' I explained that, if he couldn't deal with that, then we shouldn't be doing this, and if he really didn't enjoy watching me have sex with other guys, he had to tell me.

Just then his mobile phone went off. It was Mark asking for my number.

'No, Mark,' I heard him say. 'You can't have her phone number. Sorry, mate.'

Mark was the last threesome we ever had. It wasn't fun for Daniel any more. And, as it developed, he wasn't much fun for me, either. From being a three-a-day guy when we first met, now, eighteen months later, even with the Viagra, we were having sex once a week. Most nights he said he was too tired.

I suspected he wasn't lying. More and more, when I came home from work at six p.m., I'd find him asleep on the sofa, with the TV on, snoring. The situation became increasingly unfulfilling. The challenge of trying to turn this guy's life around, I realised, was insurmountable.

Over the next few weeks I took steps to get him out. 'Listen,' I said, 'I really don't love you any more. Our two-month-notice period is long past and nothing has changed. I'd like you to move out, Daniel.'

I had to find a way to get him to stop loving me, so I began to cheat.

Only ten minutes to go. I look at the clock: 12.50 p.m. At one I grab my briefcase and my jacket and tell my receptionist, a pretty young blonde girl with a penchant for heavy-metal music, 'I have a meeting in town. I'll be about two hours.'

Within minutes I'm off the grotty main road and removing my clothes in the changing room before heading into the sex zone – Rio's. There are two naked black guys sitting in the Jacuzzi. The bubbling water is covering up most of their bodies, but I can still tell one of them is quite overweight. He reminds me of a laughing Buddha. The bubbles can't disguise the blubber around his neck and flabby arms. The other guy is slim, muscular and hot. He's clean shaven, including his head, and I see fantastic biceps and can make out the beginning of a sculpted chest. He has big dark eyes and a welcoming face. I walk closer to the Jacuzzi to get a better look, because I'm not wearing my glasses and want to make sure my eyes aren't deceiving me. No, I think, he really is very hot. I walk up the steps to the Jacuzzi, take off my towel and step naked into the water. I've found my target.

Sometimes people aren't friendly in spas. It might be a matter of taste – You're not my type – get lost. Or it might be territorial – This is our room, get lost. I've seen guys spread out in a Jacuzzi meant for six, not to mention sex, so that it's impossible for anyone to join them without sitting on a foot. They're just rude. Luckily, these boys are in a friendly mood; otherwise it might have been a challenge to find a way to initiate a conversation with the handsome one.

'Thought you normally came on a Wednesday,' the fatty says.

'Yeah, I do, but couldn't get away from work this Wednesday,' I say. 'I *do* come on other days, you know.'

A couple of minutes later, the laughing Buddha announces he's off to the sauna, leaving me and the hottie in the tub together. I've got a little over an hour to get this guy into one of the relaxation rooms and have an orgasm. It shouldn't be too difficult. I position myself so I'm directly across from him.

'I'm Sam,' he says.

'Suzanne.'

'Nice to meet you, Suzanne. I haven't seen you here before.'

'I usually come at Wednesday lunchtime,' I explained. 'As you heard. This is the first time I've been on a Friday.' I look meaningfully into his eyes. 'I'll have to come more often.'

We discuss what we do for a living. He's a property developer with a sideline in making corporate videos. He is sweet and relaxed and I like him instantly. A few minutes more of this casual chit-chat passes, then I say, 'Fancy going upstairs?'

'Really? Wow. Sure.' He seems surprised, perhaps taken aback that I'm so direct.

I'm in.

I learnt that the direct approach usually works. As my mother taught me, 'If you don't ask, you don't get.' She was talking about a waiter bringing us an extra round of bread. I learnt to adapt that advice to satisfy my needs. When you've only got an hour to get laid, small talk is a waste of time.

The first time I went to Rio's was with Daniel, a year earlier, on his birthday. I'd asked him what he wanted as a present, and he told me, 'I want sex with lots of strangers. Organise it.'

As I am not Heidi Fleiss, I didn't quite know what to do. But then I recalled a leaflet I'd picked up at an erotica exhibition I'd attended as a joke with some girlfriends; it was now tacked to the kitchen bulletin board, hidden behind my children's school-holiday dates. What caught my eye and made me keep it was the small type: 'Couples' Night'. Although the brochure didn't proclaim it, it was apparent that meant 'Swingers' Night'. Since it was just down the road from my house, we decided to check it out, more out of curiosity than anything else. We figured that, even if it was crap, we'd have a laugh. I promised Daniel that if the place was a bust, we could come home and I would make up for the lack of performance art by performing a few tricks of my own.

It wasn't immediately apparent to us, on that first visit, where the alleged swinging was taking place. After sitting at the bar for twenty minutes and seeing people stew in the Jacuzzi, we noticed a couple being buzzed through a door that led upstairs. We asked a bearded guy, an old hippy sitting next to us, what was upstairs. 'Ooooh, you need an open mind to go up there.' That was our signal.

We climbed two flights of stairs, passing the relaxation rooms and discovered an orgy, with about twenty people in various intriguing configurations. There was a large white woman with drooping tits and a hefty belly in the middle of the room, on all fours, being fucked by three men, one in each hole. Sofas lined the walls. Most of the people on them were middle-aged men being sucked off by their partners or, in a few cases, by younger women who could have been hookers. These women were far too attractive, I thought, to be the partner of some fat hairy white guy, and I wondered if the men had hired the girls for the night and brought them to Rio's.

Swingers clubs attract a real cross-section of humanity. Imagine fucking everyone in the Tube carriage on the way to work. There's always a pretty girl, a hunky boy and everyone else is fairly average. Rio's is just like life, except it's full of people who made the leap, got over their fears – if they ever had any – and take off their clothes and perform sex acts with strangers in public. These clubs are heaven for most men, who are happy to be getting so much pussy. They just want a hole to fill. It's different for women, who often can't relate to a cock on its own. They want them attached to men with beauty or bodies or brains, preferably all three; otherwise, they must close their eyes and concentrate on a fantasy to get off.

That first night at Rio's, Daniel got his birthday wish when we got friendly with a gorgeous Spanish girl with perfect tits and a French woman who didn't know how to suck cock to save her life (though we enjoyed watching her try). For six months after that, we were Saturday-night regulars – until the night I pointed out a black guy's twelve-inch erection as he and it emerged from a Jacuzzi. Daniel said angrily, 'If that's what you want, you shouldn't be with me.' He had been sensitive about his size ever since the day he asked how he measured up against my previous lovers.

'Well, truthfully,' I said, 'I'm used to much bigger.'

'You know, Suzanne,' he said, 'sometimes it really is better to lie.'

'Darling, if you want me to lie, you shouldn't have asked.'

Sam and I get to the door that leads upstairs and he asks the receptionist to buzz us in. She flashes me a dirty look, as if to say, 'I see you've found another victim.' It takes her about thirty seconds to reach the buzzer that is about two inches from her hand.

Sam and I find an empty room. We take off the towels we've been wearing around our waists and spread them on top of the mat. We embrace and kiss. His body is even better than I had anticipated – pronounced abs, athletic thighs, narrow hips that offset broad shoulders. He's hard. I sit on the platform bed and take his cock in my mouth. It tastes slightly of chlorine, is about nine inches long and thick. If I had more time, I'd stay down there longer. Sucking cock, especially a big gorgeous black cock, is one of my favourite things to do, and fortunately I'm told I'm very good at it. I have Frank to thank for that. He taught me everything there is to know about sucking cock. Before I met him, I didn't have a clue. I thought the nerve endings were at the base of the shaft – that, I assumed, was the significance of the movie *Deep Throat*.

Once, during a weekend visit to New York, we were in bed and I noticed that yet another of my blowjobs was making Frank go limp – I didn't have much oral experience, since most men just wanted to fuck me – and he told me to stop.

'Close your eyes and relax,' he said, then explained what I needed to do to make him come. 'Imagine what it would be like if *you* had a cock.'

Now I think of blowjobs not so much as an act of love as a form of meditation, and in the same spirit in which he performed oral on me. If there were a religion for girls who like sucking cock, I'd be a convert.

Once I get into the rhythm, I lose all sense of time and place. It's just me and the cock. Actually it's more than that: the man thinks it's all about him, but, in fact, for me, it's an act of pure selfishness. I suck cock because I love it.

Frank taught me to feel every twitch, the way a man's penis gets hard and then subsides slightly when he is trying not to come. I love the responsiveness of a cock; the way it slides in and out of my mouth; the way I can make it do what I want it to do. I think about how it must feel when my tongue circles around the head and when I take it deep into my mouth until I almost gag. I slide my tongue up and down the shaft and then back into my mouth again. In my mind, I'm so connected to the man's cock, I get wetter and wetter and almost come myself, just thinking about what he must be feeling. My head moves up and down, up and down. Then I'm massaging the head of his cock again, swirling my tongue, watching and feeling him get harder and harder.

A big hard cock is a thing of beauty. I don't need to hear the words 'I love you' or 'I want to fuck you'. A man's arousal is the ultimate turn-on for me. I'm in my own world. And, lucky man, Sam is loving it.

The clock is ticking and, although I'm on an endorphin high sucking Sam's cock, my reason for spending lunchtime at Rio's is simple: I want to come. So I stop sucking. Now it's my turn. I lie down on my back and Sam crouches between my legs, inhaling my scent before darting his tongue over, around and on top of my clit. I can feel myself getting wetter.

'I want to feel your cock inside me,' I say.

I grab a condom from my kitbag, which contains my other Rio's essentials: shampoo, conditioner, massage oil, lube, a bullet vibrator and a butt plug.

I split the wrapper and roll the condom on his hard-on, making sure my mouth follows immediately, to be certain he'll stay hard enough.

I climb on top of him, slide his cock inside me, and start to grind. He's the perfect size and the perfect shape for me. Any thicker and it might be painful; any smaller and I wouldn't feel him sliding up and down inside me. We fit. He's just thick enough to feel full and long enough to reach to the end of my pussy without hurting. It feels good and I'm really enjoying this. It's a lot better than what I've got at home and makes me realise what I've been missing. I move up and down the shaft, massaging it with my pussy. He's groaning with pleasure. 'Your pussy is fantastic.'

'If you keep going,' he says, 'I'm going to come too quickly. I want to make this last.' He seems to be enjoying it as much as I am, which is to say, a bit too much. That's not the deal. The deal is, I fuck a stranger, don't get his number and never see him again. I don't want the complications of an affair. This is a snack, after all, not the main meal. Besides, I'm living with my boyfriend.

I come, and a few minutes later so does Sam. I look at my watch; an hour has gone by. I've still got to shower, dry my hair and change. We lie together for a short while, then get up off the bed, both of us soaking in sweat. The red walls are covered with beads of our sweat as well. We embrace.

That final embrace is always so much more awkward than the first. Only minutes before we were complete strangers, laying together and having sex, just like a porn fairy tale. Then, a few minutes later, we're saying our goodbyes. The words sound no different to what is said after bumping into a neighbour at the corner store.

As I turn to head back to the changing rooms, Sam says, 'So, see you next Friday, then?'

'Sounds good,' I say, smiling, even though I know it's breaking my one-shot-only rule.

Ten minutes later I'm back at my desk.

Over the next week I tell myself that going back to Rio's the next Friday is a really dumb idea. My body is telling me something else. Sam felt a lot better than Daniel does – bigger cock, better body and he likes straightforward intercourse. Hallelujah! Perhaps another bite at the apple wouldn't be so terrible, I think, telling myself it's only a lunchtime thing. I spend more time at the gym, I think. What's one hour a week? Still, I call my girlfriend Bernadette to sound her out.

'But what about Daniel?' she says. 'What about *him*?'

'It's not really cheating; it's only lunch,' I say. 'It doesn't count if it's only lunch.'

'If you say so.'

I tell her I don't even have his number, so he's more fantasy than reality at this point anyway.

I'm back at Rio's the following Friday.

Sam is there. This time we don't bother much with small talk or the Jacuzzi but head straight upstairs.

It's great, just like the first time. We part after our second perfect date with the same words as before – 'See you next Friday' – but both of us know that's not going to happen. That's not the gig. You don't go to places like Rio's if you want a relationship.

I show up the next Friday anyway. He's not there. I'm half-relieved, half-disappointed. I have sex with a middle-aged, greying man who makes me come with his fingers.

When I got home that night, Daniel said, 'I need to talk to you.' I wondered if he'd found out about my lunchtime snacks.

Daniel paused. 'I wasn't going to tell you, because you've been such a bitch recently,' he said, 'but I suppose I should. I have liver cancer. It's inoperable. The doctor says I have three to six months left. It would be really great if you'd let me stick around with you.'

I can't say I was stunned by the news. I'd had a premonition when we first met that he was unwell; this hard-living guy didn't seem the type to live to a ripe old age. Even my children had once asked over breakfast why Daniel's eyes were so yellow. Then there was the tiredness, his always falling asleep on the sofa, the length of time it took him to get over colds and the flus, and the slow disintegration of our sex life. Suddenly, it all made sense. Nonetheless, I hadn't suspected the severity of his illness.

I didn't know what I was meant to say. Part of me didn't feel anything. I hadn't felt any love for Daniel in months. Yet I knew I should cry, like in the movies. It would have been the right thing to do, the expected thing. Part of me felt sad and sorry for the man sitting opposite me. He was only forty-four years old.

Despite my anger and resentment and shock and pity, tears came to my eyes.

'I'm not sorry to go, Suzanne,' he said. 'I've done everything I wanted to do, you know.' He mentioned some early career accomplishments; said he'd seen a lot of the world as a kid; and cited the number of women he'd fucked. 'I know it sounds like something out of a chick flick, the final scene, but I've crammed more into forty-four years than most people do in eighty, and, you know what, I'm fucking tired.'

Daniel was stoic and that made me feel better about my ambivalent feelings about losing him. There was an end to our relationship in sight, even if it wasn't the kind either of us would have desired. Despite the tears, I felt relieved, then guilt at feeling relieved. Another three to six months. I wondered whether it might be longer. What if the doctors didn't get the diagnosis right and six months turns into a year? I wondered. I couldn't imagine a year of nursing someone I didn't love.

'I'm so sorry, Daniel,' I said. 'Of course you can stay.' I didn't want him to die alone.

10. BIG COCK LONDON

The doctor told Daniel that, because his liver cancer was so advanced and there was nothing they could do, his only treatment would be pain management at this point. Chemo was not recommended, as it wasn't considered worth the harsh side-effects for such minimal payoff. Still, we spent most of our time following Daniel's diagnosis ferrying back and forth to the Royal Free Hospital. Perhaps because it was a teaching hospital, doctors there seemed always to be calling Daniel in for tests.

Daniel refused to tell his family about his condition, saying he didn't want them to fuss over him. I was his sole carer and chauffeur – not roles I was born to play – and I found it emotionally exhausting. My moods veered from sadness for Daniel to anger at myself that a relationship I had tried to end a year earlier had come to this. So, while the doctors and nurses took blood samples and did MRIs and pored over X-rays, I sat in waiting rooms.

Daniel was so tired from all the tests and poking and prodding, and so bloated from the water his body could not flush through his kidneys, that just walking from the hospital reception to the oncology department might take a half-hour. He was too proud to take a wheelchair. Even putting on his shoes took a quarter of an hour. The nurses came round to my house one day and, seeing the stairs, told Daniel that soon he would have to move to a hospice. I was relieved. I had already decided I didn't want my children to see Daniel die in my house, and he had offered to move to a hospice when it was clear that he was close to death. Now the deadline was being imposed on us.

Soon after Daniel's diagnosis, we were on a visit to the hospital and asked his doctor to prescribe Viagra. We thought it was the least the NHS could do. We hadn't had sex in months and I knew sex was the one thing Daniel really wanted. Daniel had told me it was only when he could no longer perform in bed that he had decided to go to the doctor. It wasn't his falling asleep all the time, or his rapid weight gain, or even the alarming shade of yellow his eyes had become. It was that my world-class blowjobs no longer had an effect. 'You were the only one in the world who made me hard,' he told me, 'and, when I couldn't get it up for you any longer, that's when I knew I was really sick.'

As sex was what he'd always lived for, I wanted to give Daniel the one thing that gave him joy, so I didn't think that mentioning the Viagra was such a big deal. Apparently it was. The doctor looked at me, shocked, as if he couldn't believe someone could ask for something so base at such a sensitive time.

'I just think his last few months should be as pleasurable for him as possible,' I explained.

'I don't really want to do that right now,' the doctor replied. 'Let's see how the treatment goes first.'

'What fucking treatment?' I was disgusted. 'According to you, he doesn't have much time. This is what he really likes.'

The doctor was appalled. 'Let's revisit this when your boyfriend returns for his next visit.'

It took several more trips to hospital and another two doctors before we finally found one who was sympathetic. 'Of course,' he said, and immediately wrote out a prescription. But by then it was too late; Daniel was too sick for sex.

We hadn't had sex in months, anyway, and my brief Rio's phase ended when my Florence Nightingale phase began. The idea of sex with others just didn't feel right when on my mind was the boyfriend at home, dying in my bed.

But one Sunday afternoon, overwhelmed by grief, constrained by my lack of freedom, feeling imprisoned in my own home, I rebelled. I went to the computer and pulled up SwingingHeaven, a website that a guy at Rio's had told me about one afternoon as we chatted, post coitus, in the steam room. I just want to get fucked, I thought. I went into the photo adverts, pressed 'Search' and typed *big + cock + London*. Up popped Greg.

Aside from his big cock, I didn't know much more about him. The picture showed a man who looked about forty, with very short blond hair and a trim goatee similar to Daniel's. It looked like he had a decent body – fit but not overly muscular. His cock looked as advertised, very big – long and thick.

Experienced, very sensible, clean, tested and discrete guy, 38 years old. Fit, athletic build, with a nice thick 8+ cock. Available for the pleasure of single ladies. Confident, assertive and considerate, very broad-minded and good company. I live in north London and can travel for daytime or evening meetings. Distance or short notice no problem.

It sounded just what the doctor ordered. I sent an email, saying I was living with someone but asking if he fancied an afternoon meeting the following Friday, enclosing my picture. He wrote back that day and said he'd be delighted. We arranged to hook up at Rio's, conveniently located close to where we both lived.

Daniel went into the hospice two days later, and died on Friday, three days after that. His mother called to tell me the news as I was giving the kids their breakfast.

The wait was over. I'd done my share of grieving during the previous two months. I felt sad but also relieved that I no longer had to play the part of the grieving girlfriend. I drove to the hospice one last time and paid my condolences to Daniel's parents and brothers, who were gathered around his bedside. Daniel was lying on the bed, a clean white sheet pulled up to his chin, with two small flowers lying on either side of the pillow. An odd touch, I thought. I had never seen a dead person before and wondered if the flowers were part of the ritual. Daniel had a smile on his face. He looked peaceful. I went to the bed and kissed his forehead. It was ice cold. It was unsettling to think that someone I'd spent so many hot moments with was now so cold. 'Goodbye, sweetheart,' I said. I hugged his family. We cried together. A half-hour later I left the hospice and went back to work. I told my staff that Daniel was dead, crying some more as I shared the news, and then took the rest of the day off. I told my ex-husband what happened and asked him to pick up the kids after school and take them for the weekend.

Part of me felt I should cancel my meeting with Greg. The other part of me wanted to move on and stop crying and grieving and feeling sad. I drove to Rio's.

Greg was waiting in the reception area when I arrived. Thankfully, he looked just like his picture; I was not in the mood for more unpleasant surprises. We kissed hello and went to our changing rooms. I removed my clothes, trying, as I removed each layer, to distance myself further from what had transpired that morning.

When I looked at myself naked in the mirror, I felt free. I was back in the game, and this time I wasn't cheating.

I grabbed the white towel, tightened it round my body and stepped into the club. Greg was at the bar already, drinking a cup of tea. 'You fancy a steam?' I asked.

'Sounds good to me,' he said, arching an eyebrow. 'Lead the way.'

I took him to the hottest steam room at the end of the hall. It was fairly quiet. There was a handful of men there, none of whom I recognised.

We removed our towels, laid them on the tiled bench and sat next to each other. The room was enveloped in steam and it was hard to make out the contours of Greg's body or to see his cock. But the heat felt great. 'This is just what I need,' he said.

You don't know the half of it, I thought. I wasn't interested in telling him about my morning. I didn't want him to feel sorry for me. I didn't want condolences or to answer questions about how my boyfriend had died. I didn't want to spoil the moment.

I asked Greg what he did for a living and he said he was a musician. He played the bass and worked as a recording engineer and sometime record producer. He had been in a fairly well-known band in the 80s, made a bit of money and now had a small recording studio in town.

'We have a lot in common,' I said. I explained that I had sung in a trio back in my twenties and now worked as a publicist and had a number of music clients. I learnt he produced a record for a band my company was publicising at the time. He was easy to talk to – a relief, as I'd been off the scene for a while and was feeling slightly nervous. We talked about work instead of talking dirty. At least at first.

I didn't want to be too obvious about the focus of my afternoon but, as he'd made a point of advertising his cock size, I figured he probably was expecting me to confirm the authenticity of his ad at some point. 'I'm getting really hot,' I said. 'Shall we check out the Jacuzzi?'

He followed me into the pool, and both of us sat in silence while the hot water bubbled around us. It disguised what was down below. 'Do you mind if I touch your cock?' I asked.

'I thought you'd never ask.'

I put my hand under the water and discovered that he was already hard. I stroked the shaft, feeling the engorged blood vessels. His cock was at least eight inches long, perhaps nine, and had a well-pronounced thick head.

Thank God for Google, I said to myself. Big Cock London, indeed. I wondered what it would feel like inside me.

Greg's hands went under the water and he started playing with my pussy. We had the Jacuzzi to ourselves. Still we sat in silence. I didn't feel like talking much anyway. I wanted to get fucked. 'Shall we go upstairs?' I said.

I led him to the red room in the corner, the only relaxation room I knew that came with a pillow. That day, I wanted the extra comfort. We laid the towels on the mat, as I'd done so many times before. Greg lay down next to me. His cock flopped heavily on to the mat.

I put his cock in my mouth and he indicated his pleasure with a groan. It was so thick, it was a strain to open my mouth as wide as necessary. He held the back of my neck, pushing his cock further down my throat, saying, 'That's good. Take it all in.'

I felt myself getting wet, enjoying the domination. After months of keeping up the act, having to be the strong one all the time, I wanted to relinquish control. Let someone else take charge, I thought. I was happy to let Greg do what he wanted with me, content to give in completely to his desire. I sucked his cock for half an hour, varying the intensity of the pressure my mouth put on it, varying the speed, licking the head, the shaft. I found myself back in a familiar meditative state. The rhythm was my mantra as my mouth went up and down, up and down on his penis. Despite the size of his cock, the rhythm lulled me into a state of complete relaxation, and slowly I was able to get his cock to the back of my throat. It was liberating.

By the end of the half-hour, I was dripping wet. Greg reached for my pussy. 'Lie down on your back,' he ordered me, grabbing a condom from his kitbag. He put the condom on skilfully, then plunged into me rapidly. I felt the head of his cock hit against the back wall of my vagina, stretching me. If it hurt, I didn't notice. I closed my eyes and wrapped my legs around his back, pulling him further into me with every stroke. I didn't think about coming; I didn't think about anything except that big hard cock inside me. 'You feel so good.'

He said, 'I want to fuck you for hours.' And he did.

We manoeuvred ourselves into as many positions as was possible on a 3×6 gym mat. His sweat dripped all over me. When he came up my ass, it seemed to last for five minutes. I could feel his cock pulsating inside me as wave after wave of pleasure ran through his body. His whole body trembled. Unlike so many men who become agitated when they come, Greg seemed to be in a trance as he shot. It was a little frightening to witness. I remember thinking, I hope he's all right.

He kept his cock inside my ass while we lay down together. I'd come once already, but feeling his cock soften in my ass made me horny. I grabbed the tiny vibrator from my kitbag and used it on my clit. I could feel Greg's cock stiffen again, and ten minutes later he came once more, timed to my own orgasm.

'Do you realise we've been fucking for, like, three hours?' I said.

'Tantric,' he said, smirking.

This was my first swinging date that lasted more than a lunch hour, but I liked Greg and I didn't want to be alone that day. After we showered and got dressed, I said, 'Do you have any plans now?'

'No,' he said.

I invited him to an early dinner in Camden Town, then we drove back to mine and took off our clothes almost as soon as we got through the door. We fucked all night.

He was impressively unexhausted and could control his orgasms so that I was always the one to come first. I've scored, I thought. I wanted no-hassle fun and that's exactly what I got.

'This was great,' I said to Greg the next day as he got ready to leave. 'Do you do this kind of thing often?'

'Not usually with single girls,' he said. He told me he had a girlfriend who wasn't into swinging herself but got off on hearing his stories. He said his usual thing was to meet up with couples on the side, pairs looking for another guy to service the wife. 'I've got a regular thing going with four couples, been seeing them all for years,' he said. 'What I've been looking for is a single woman who'll go to swingers clubs and parties with me.'

He explained that, as a lone guy on the swinging scene, he often couldn't get in to places alone. 'Interested?'

'Let me know when the next party is,' I said.

In twenty-four hours I'd lost a boyfriend and picked up a swinging partner. I was on a new path and knew where I was going.

'How do you keep track of them all?' My girlfriend Bernadette thought I was mad. 'I barely have enough time for one guy, never mind four.'

'Four guys is nothing,' I told her. 'I have a diary. I slot them in.' It made it easy, I explained. I didn't have all the usual girlfriend problems, all the things chicks worry about: when I'd see him next, whether he'd phone me, how much he liked me. I didn't have to get involved in their lives, I told her. 'I just look in my diary and see who I'm going to meet the next day.'

Following my return to Rio's the day Daniel died, Greg and I got together every two or three weeks and went to swinging parties. In between our dates I arranged 'meetings' with other guys I plucked off SwingingHeaven. There was no shortage of big thick cocks attached to guys who liked using them. I'd finally found my world.

I'd typed 'Big Cock London' into SwingingHeaven's search engine for a reason and, after Greg, I had to admit what I always suspected: I'm a size queen.

Pre-Daniel, I thought I could snag a part-time relationship with a dream man the usual ways – newspaper personals, online dating, Soho House – and usually ended up disappointed. Outwardly, these men ticked a lot of my boxes. They looked good, had brains, a decent job, usually a sense of humour. But once they removed their clothes, they didn't measure up for one reason or another.

Now, on my list of priorities, the cock came first. Face and bod were next, followed by brains and personality. For once, everyone was honest, too. The focus was on sex. No more pretence about wanting to find a lifelong partner, fall in love, live happily ever after.

The trick was not to care about any of my fuck buddies too much. I learnt to compartmentalise my emotions. I liked the men in my diary enough to spend an evening with them but not a lifetime. All the stuff that bogs down relationships, the things that doom or take the fun out of them, no longer applied. No brains? No problem. No money? Who cared? Not many men will turn down a relationship that requires showing up every couple of weeks and getting fucked, with minimal contact in between. They seemed to think, 'It doesn't come more perfect than this', and so did I. 'See you in a couple of weeks,' they'd say, as they walked out the door smiling.

While Bernadette remained perpetually saddened that she could never meet Mr Right, or even Mr Almost Right, I became a case in point of a woman who happily accepted the limitations. In the fifteen years I have known her, I've watched Bernadette lurch from one catastrophic relationship to another – the cokehead whose habit she tolerated until he became so paranoid he punched her in the face for supposedly flirting with another guy; the clean freak who made her change her sheets every time they had sex. As for me, I found freedom not just from not having to take care of a sick boyfriend, but from not having to take care of any man.

I quickly discovered that, just as at Rio's, I was the belle of the ball. The ratio of men to women on SwingingHeaven was about 250:1, and many of the women weren't even real; they were gay men looking for cock shots.

I felt more mature, and for once 'mature' was not a euphemism for 'old', and feeling older was not a bad thing. When I was younger, it seemed I was always waiting for the phone to ring. Now, I was the one making the calls and, unlike in the past, there were few rejections. Honesty came with this maturity. Everyone who I slept with knew the score – that they weren't the only one and would never be. And I stopped trying to fit my dates into boxes in which they obviously didn't belong.

My first date off SwingingHeaven, after Greg, might have been a keeper in my youth. His name was Anthony and he was a hottie. His biography sounded like that of a character in a porn movie. In fact, he could have starred in a porn movie himself. He was a policeman with a fantastic body and a big cock. He had thick dark Italian hair that he swept off his forehead, long eyelashes, big white teeth, big eyes and huge cheekbones. And he was horny as hell. He was fun in bed and made me laugh in and out of it. He was a great kisser who loved to kiss. He also had irregular working hours, a young daughter on whom he doted and a salary one-third my own. But it was great to see him once a month. Sometimes I'd send him a text message to ask if he'd be around that coming weekend, and he'd text back something dirty, like telling me about the hard-on he had while driving around the city in his Vauxhall Astra thinking about me. I learnt that scheduling him in more often than once a month would have been impossible. Anthony frequently broke dates at the last minute, when called back to work or too tired to play. He never would fit into my nine-to-five life.

Same went for Dave, the taxi driver who worked nights. He was perfect for a three a.m. quickie in the back of a cab. It was fun to run outside in the middle of the night to give him a blowjob, dressed only in a negligée and a pair of froufrou slippers. But he was not the kind of man to treat me to a fancy dinner; in fact, fancy dinners, like nights at the Barbican or concerts at the Royal Festival Hall or subtitled movies at the Renoir Cinema, were not his kind of thing at all. If he were a fixture of my world, dreary Saturday-night dates with the telly would have been guaranteed, given that was his busiest shift. Still, his blue eyes twinkled under the streetlights and he was the most amazing fuck. No sooner would Dave come inside me than he'd be hard again, and go for another round or two. I'd never met a man who could come four times in a row without stopping, pausing only to change a condom when it swelled too much with spunk. I asked him if every fuck was so heroic. 'Only when I'm with someone as horny as you, Suzanne,' he said.

My third date off SwingingHeaven was a beefy landscape gardener named Julio, whom I'd meet at Rio's on Wednesdays at eleven a.m., two hours before his weekly client meeting. He was a cute guy in his late thirties, with dark-brown hair and a massive chest. He was about 6'4" and had a really thick cock that he loved having me suck. And he was great at oral in return. His inner Lothario was frustrated, given that, on the rare times his wife had sex with him, she would come within two minutes, he said, and then roll over. He was looking for someone who enjoyed sex as much as he did and was equally willing to devote some time to it. Unfortunately, in addition to a wife, he had a couple of kids and lived up north.

I was relishing my newfound freedom, not only with the guys I got off the web, but also with Big Cock London Greg. It was an eye-opener exploring the swinging scene with him. 'Hi,' he said one day. 'I just heard about this club in north London called OurPlace4Fun. You want to check it out?'

We made a date for that coming Friday.

Greg picked me up at ten, wearing black leather trousers, a tight black rubber shirt and black Tony Lama cowboy boots. I had on the same leopard-print dress I wore in New York when Frank took me to my first swingers club, plus black fishnet stockings and my favourite fuck-me shoes.

We spent fifteen minutes driving up and down the street in Alexandra Palace where OurPlace was supposed to be, but didn't see anything that looked like a swingers club, just a row of shops, an Indian restaurant, a closed newsagent and an off-licence where underage kids were hanging out, trying to buy booze. I phoned the number I'd pulled off the club's website and was directed down a narrow alley with rows of garages on either side. Suddenly, just as we were turning around and about to leave the alley, thinking we'd gone to the wrong place, a door opened and light poured into the street.

'I think you're looking for us?' said the doorman.

We walked up a long steep flight of stairs and paid our £20 through a window to a blonde woman sitting in a sheer red slip. She buzzed us through a second door and we entered a large dimly lit room. A bar was on the left side, and red and green neon outlined the ceiling. There didn't seem to be many people there. Beyond the bar we could see a number of smaller rooms but not whether anyone was in any of them. Greg gave the wine bottle that we'd brought with us – the website described the club as BYOB – to a man who exchanged it for a cloakroom tag. 'You're number seven,' he said archly.

I hope that doesn't mean there are only six other couples ahead of us, I thought.

'Would you like me to pour a glass now,' asked the bartender, 'or would you like to save this for later?' I liked the way he winked and his cheeky smile.

We decided to have a glass, and when we finished I said to Greg, 'Shall we have a look around?'

We wandered through empty rooms and soon saw why they and the front bar were so quiet. All the action was going on in the Grope Room, a tiny 5×8 space with a barred window reminiscent of a prison cell on the right side and, on either side of that, a half-dozen glory holes, four-inch circles cut into the wall just below waist height.

'So this is where everyone's been hiding,' said Greg.

There must have been eight men squashed inside that small room, all with hard cocks protruding from their trousers, while Lisa, the club's hostess, whom I recognised from the website, was doing her best to accommodate them all in one way or another.

'Go on,' I said to Greg. I unzipped his trousers and pushed him into the bars that separated him and the boys from Lisa on the other side. His thickening cock, half erect and already the largest in the group, caught her attention and she stopped what she was doing with everyone else to focus on Greg. I was standing behind him, watching as Lisa began jerking him off. I felt a hand lift up my dress and explore between my legs. After a few minutes of touching me, I heard a voice say, 'Can I fuck you?'

'Only if you have a rubber,' I said, without turning around.

'Of course,' said the voice. Soon I felt a prodding. I reached my hand back to make sure he had put on the condom and, satisfied, let him slip inside me. I never turned to see what he looked like, and instead focused my attention on Greg, who was now fucking Lisa through the bars.

She came a few minutes later and Greg pulled out. 'Nice to meet you, Lisa,' he said, laughing.

'Likewise,' she answered, smiling.

I pulled away from the man behind me and said, 'That's enough for now.' Then I said to Lisa, 'Can I have a go in there?'

'Sure, darling, be my guest.' She unlocked the door to her side of the Grope Room and I walked in, taking her place. She kissed me on the lips and said, 'Have fun.'

I removed my dress while appraising the row of cocks in front of me, and pulled a bottle of lube out of my handbag. I poured a little juice into my palm and took turns playing with three cocks. I could feel the adrenalin surge through my body as I sucked one guy and jerked off the other two. It felt as if all the sexual energy in the room was being transferred to me. It gave me a sense of power and control.

I was sucking a man off when I heard him say, 'I want to fuck you.' I didn't say anything. I pulled a condom out of my bag, slipped it on his cock, turned around, then felt him push his cock into my ass.

'Slow down!' I said. 'I have to get ready.' I'd assumed he was going to enter the traditional way. I was wrong. I let my muscles relax and soon felt them give way to his cock. He began pushing inside until he was fully in. I returned to jerking off his neighbours, this time with my back to them. It was so horny, for all of us. The guy fucking me did not take long to come, and when he pulled out another took his place. I stayed in that room for an hour.

This is every middle-aged woman's fantasy, I thought. A middle-aged woman and a grope box: what a combination.

I didn't have to look at them and I didn't have to speak to them if I didn't want to. After forty-three years, I'd grown tired of small talk. It doesn't get better than this.

I put on my dress and walked out of the room. Greg was in a gang bang in another part of the club. I tapped him on the shoulder and said, 'Come on. We're going.'

We spent many such nights on the scene. Women would come up to us in sex clubs after watching us together and say, 'You guys are so horny. How long have you been together?'

We'd tell them we weren't together, that we only met for sex.

'That's so cool,' they'd say.

After a while, I began to wonder if it really was.

Greg and I had a lot of spectacular sexcapades, but after six months I worried I might never have a real relationship again. It wasn't that I wanted one. It was that I began to fear I'd never be capable of having one again. My sex life with Frank had always been about portraying myself as a woman who didn't give a shit about him, who just enjoyed sex for its own sake and used him as a human dildo, who didn't care about anyone else. I hated that role at the time. Now, I found, it had become my life. And, fun as it was, part of me suspected it wasn't healthy.

11. MY TANTRIC TEMPTATION

It was one a.m. at Soho House. I was sitting with friends, perched on the edge of a large brown sofa in the top-floor Kitchen Bar. Howard, a TV producer with a foot fetish, had been stroking my purple Buddhahood stiletto ankle boots for the past hour. 'I wish they made these in *my* size,' he said. 'I had a pair of shoes just like this back in the 80s, and I've been looking for something similar ever since.'

You're a complete fruitcake, I said to myself. I said to him, 'Sorry, darling. You're out of luck. These are the last pair and I'm not selling.'

Then Oliver walked in. He was an older man, about 55, whom I'd fancied for ages. I'd lusted after him for so many years I'd almost forgotten about him. He was just part of the background, always there in my head, tucked away under 'Would Love Some Of That'. It wasn't an obsessive attraction.

We had met only a handful of times. We were introduced at a friend's fiftieth birthday party at the Cobden Club in Kensal

Rise. The party was held in a huge open room, all dark-wood panelling with one very long dark-wood bar at one end and sofas and little tables and chairs at the other. He was talking with someone I recognised – Yasmin, the wife of my friend Aidan. I was having an affair with Frank at the time and was in a state of high excitement, having just returned from a weekend fuckfest in New York. I walked up to Yasmin, whom I hadn't seen in six months, for a catch-up, and she introduced me to a filmmaker named Oliver. 'Nice to meet you,' he said in a deep resonant voice, smooth like a perfectly aged red wine. It was the kind of voice I could listen to for hours.

He wasn't my usual type, being just a couple of inches, rather than a full head, taller than me and at least ten years older. He had short slightly spiked grey hair and a grey beard and moustache he trimmed close to the face. He had delicate features and kind blue eyes under gold wire-rimmed specs. I thought he was incredibly handsome and refined and sexy. Afterwards, we would run into each other, usually at the House, and I discovered he was friends with many of my friends. 'How's it going, Suzanne?' he'd ask when I'd see him. 'Fine, thanks,' I'd answer. And that was about it unless we found ourselves together in a group. Then I could hover, listen to him tell stories about the latest film he was directing and look into his lovely eyes. When I didn't see him, I didn't think about him; but, when I did see him, I was reminded of how attractive I found him. It wasn't just the way he looked, although that was a large part of it. It was his maturity and confidence, the air he exuded of someone who didn't have anything to prove. He was grounded – the antithesis of Daniel, who couldn't walk into a room without making sure everyone noticed him.

I pulled my shoe out of Howard's hand, stood up and walked straight up to Oliver. It could have been that Oliver made me feel especially relaxed that night. It could have been the four Bloody Marys I'd drunk while waiting for an investment banker to show up – who I later learnt had missed his flight from

Geneva. Or it could have been that I was especially horny and now disappointed that my banker man wasn't going to come through. But, when I saw him, I thought, This is my chance. If you want this guy, Suzanne, it's now or never.

'Hello, Suzanne,' he said. 'How are you?'

'I'm fine,' I said. 'Can I come home with you and give you a fabulous blowjob?' I'd moved on from my almost-virginal-sounding chat-up line – 'I really must kiss you now' – and was enjoying great success with this even-more-direct approach. I leant towards Oliver and kissed him. He grabbed my ass, pulled me towards him and put his tongue in my mouth.

'I don't see why not.'

'Great,' I said. 'Then I'll catch up with you later.' We each hung out in our separate orbits for an hour or so, but as I circulated through the L-shaped room I kept an eye on him to make sure my reservation still held. The club filled up with six-foot model types, who began clustering around the handsome man with the wire-rimmed glasses. I'd been waiting at the House since ten, for the date that was not to be. But, because Oliver had just arrived at one, I knew that, despite my proposition, he wanted to hang out for a while. If I wanted to go home with him, I had to stick it out till closing time, still a couple of hours away. I didn't mind waiting.

I went back to the foot fetishist. I put my foot on the arm of the chair and said, 'Here you go.' Howard continued to rub my feet as other people I knew came by and chatted. Finally, at closing, I removed my foot from Howard again and said goodbye. I found Oliver downstairs at the Circle Bar, leaning against the bar talking to some guy.

'Ready to go?'

He looked surprised to see me. 'Oh, were you serious about that blowjob?' he said quietly to me.

'Of course I was serious,' I said. 'C'mon, my car's outside.'

We walked across the street to the China Town Car Park and, when we reached my car, I said, 'So, where are we going?'

'Shepherd's Bush.'

Even as I drove through London, I wasn't certain I'd serve as anything more than a taxi service. We had never spoken much. Tonight's brief conversation was the longest we'd ever had. I still didn't think he quite believed I was serious, even though he was in the car with me. But when we got to his flat, a purpose-built 1960s housing estate off the Goldhawk Road, not quite what I had expected a film director to be living in, he said, 'Are you really coming in?'

'What,' I said, 'did you really think I was joking? You want your blowjob, don't you?'

He laughed. 'Well, you had better come in then.'

I parked my car in his garage after he moved some things around to make room for it.

We climbed three flights of outside stairs to reach his flat. He opened the door and, as soon as it shut behind us, we kissed. His hand went between my thighs and ripped off the fishnets I was wearing. They were ruined, but the gesture was hot. He grabbed a camera that was sitting on the kitchen worktop. I bent over, facing a full-length mirror in his lounge, and hoisted up my skirt to give him a memento of the evening.

'You're very naughty,' he said.

'I know,' I said, laughing. Then I hoisted myself up on the kitchen sink and he went down on me. I didn't want to spoil the moment but, after a few minutes, I said, 'Um, hold that thought. I really have to use the toilet. Where is it?'

'I'll show you.' He opened a door for me and stood in the bathroom entrance, watching. OK, I thought, if you want to watch me take a pee, watch me pee. Just as I was about to pull some toilet paper off the roll, Oliver reached between my legs, wiped the urine on to his hands and smelt the scent. I wasn't expecting that. Then we moved to the bedroom and fucked and kissed. He fell asleep with his arms wrapped around me. The next morning we sat in bed drinking tea, listening to Radio 4 and playing with each other. Later, lying in his bath together, he said, 'Would you mind shaving my balls?'

We were so comfortable together it didn't seem such an unusual request. I felt like we were old friends, or a couple that had been together for ages. I thought it incredibly trusting of him, too, and felt almost honoured.

'Has anyone ever done this for you before?' I asked.

'No, you are the first. You will be careful, won't you?'

I lathered his balls with shaving cream and he passed me a razor. Carefully pulling the skin taut, I shaved his balls, a section at a time, while Oliver stroked his cock. It was a turn-on for both of us. When I finished, we carried on lying in the bath together and masturbated till we both came.

'Are you hungry?' he said.

'Starving.'

Oliver made me a big English breakfast. Other than Daniel and Søren, few men had ever cooked for me before.

'Have you ever seen any of my films?' he said. 'Do you even know what I do?'

'No,' I admitted. 'I knew you worked in films or TV or something, but I've never seen your stuff, no.'

'Do you have some time? I'll put something on.'

I told him I'd have loved to, but had to get back home. I had housework to do.

He looked slightly disappointed, like he'd thought we were going to settle in for the weekend, like an old married couple. And I would have, too, but for my domestic duties. Hanging out with Oliver felt comfortable and natural, but, I feared, I'd set the tone of our relationship with that bold offer of sex.

'You're a free spirit, Suzanne,' he said, as he opened his front door. 'The man who catches you would have to be much more...' He didn't finish the sentence. I wondered what he had planned to say. Much more *what* than he was? Wilder? More confident? Better in bed?

I suspected someone like Oliver would never consider having a relationship with someone like me. He saw me as a sexual adventuress – someone with whom he could live out his fantasies, not as a stay-at-home girlfriend who'd cook him dinners. Even though we'd had the most glorious twenty-four hours together, he hadn't made me come. And I suspected that didn't bother him. I was the free spirit, the fantasy girl, and, when you're someone's fantasy, the focus is not really on you. Pleasing me, I suspected, wasn't part of his plan.

I had wanted Oliver for so long and, now that I'd been in his bed, I felt a little sad. Over the years, I'd fantasised about this handsome man with the gold-rimmed glasses – as a partner, not just a fuck. Those twenty-four hours knocked me back to reality. Despite my disappointment, I felt relief. I'd moved him forward in my mind. If it's the fantasy girl you want, I thought as I drove myself home, then that's what I'll give you. It's enough for now. It felt like a step forward, somehow. At least we were no longer acquaintances.

It was hard not to offend when I told my single girlfriends how easy it was to achieve the UK standard – as reported by the *Sun* newspaper – of three times a week, without having a boyfriend. My girlfriends probably were not coming anywhere near that benchmark themselves, and thus were doubly sore. It didn't seem right, therefore, to tell them that too much sex with too many people can take a toll.

After a year of group sex, anonymous encounters and regular fuck buddies, the memories of everyone I had been with began to merge together. I could barely distinguish a session with one man from another. My mind had disconnected from the action, and I realised I was one small step away from becoming a professional. That is, it wasn't about doing it for money; it was that sometimes, in my head, I wasn't with the person I was with. While I was being fucked by Greg or Oliver or Tim or Anthony or Dave or whoever, I was living out a different porn fantasy in my head, usually one that did not involve the person I was actually with.

According to my friend Hannah, who has seen a lot of action herself, this is a common problem. We were sitting in a bar in Portobello, having a drink after work, when she said, 'I've tried

S&M, asphyxiation, lesbianism, bisexuality, swinging, even being hung by my skin just for the endorphin rush.'

That got my attention.

Sipping her glass of wine, she said, 'You know, now I need to play out an entire costume drama in my head, complete with a full-scale army in uniform, wounded hero and distraught heroine, before I can get even close to coming. You can't imagine how boring it is or how long it takes.'

'I know what you mean,' I concurred. I told her about a guy I'd met off the web who couldn't make me come. He told me to knock the porn fantasies out of my mind when having sex with people and to try replacing them with straightforward dirty talk with the guy I was with, actually looking that person in the eye. 'He said, "You don't need all that shit to come, just a hard cock and some dirty talk."'

'Yeah, I've tried that,' Hannah said. 'I've also tried Neuro-linguistic Programming and Primal Therapy. Nothing works. I wish I could just find a vibrator that could pull my hair and spank me. Then I wouldn't need men at all.'

She was only twenty-five and she'd already done it all. I felt sorry for her. 'When I was your age,' I said, 'all I had to do was think, Hey, I'm getting fucked! and I'd come. Now I need to lay out a gang bang in my head just to get me there. It's a real bore.'

This really hit home the time Big Cock London Greg and I met up one Friday afternoon at Rio's. We were having sex in one of the red rooms and I was on top. He wasn't staying hard. 'So, what's up with you today?' I said. 'You don't seem your usual perky self.'

'Oh, I'm a little tired,' he said. 'I was in Essex this morning visiting this woman I know, the one whose husband works downstairs while I fuck her up the ass in her bedroom.'

'Oh, yes. That one. So what you're telling me is that I'm number two today and it's only one o'clock.'

'Yeah.'

I felt deflated. I knew he serviced other women, but it had never occurred to me I was not his number one – not as in first in his heart, but not part of the production line either. 'Maybe we should just call it quits for today,' I said. 'Suddenly, I'm not in the mood.'

We went downstairs and showered; I knew I wouldn't be ringing him for a while. I don't mind him having other women, I thought as I showered. I just don't want to be the second woman of the day. Sure, we were fuck buddies, but I wanted to feel at least a little special. I didn't want to be Friday's girl number two. Suddenly, I didn't want to be the girl that takes a cock in her mouth and one up her ass at the same time. I wanted real intimacy, I realised, something that lasted longer than a lunch-hour break.

Shortly afterwards I ran into my girlfriend Tania in a pub in Soho. 'How's your harem?' she said. 'Still enjoying the swinging?'

'Not really. I'm bored by all of them,' I said, and explained how it had become so predictable. 'Always the same desperate middle-aged guy wanting to wank all over me. Or the married ones. They're fine for a couple of dates until you have to talk to them, and then you become their counsellor and have to hear about the problems at home. It's a drag.'

'I can imagine,' she said. Tania presents a radio programme about sex, and I figured, if anyone knew what I was talking about, she did. 'Have you ever tried tantric?' she asked.

'What, you mean six hours of staying still, locked together? Trudie-and-Sting sex?'

All I knew about tantric was what I'd read in the super-market tabloids. It sounded vaguely spiritual. I'd always thought of myself as a bit of a hippy, and God knows a bit of spirituality, after a year of nonspiritual anonymous sex, probably couldn't hurt.

Tania mentioned a woman named Jahnet de Light, who had been on her radio show. 'She gives tantric lessons. I think you'd really like her. And she lives near you in north London.' She promised to pass on Jahnet's contact info.

Tania sent me Jahnet's email address the next day, and straight away I sent off a note. I didn't know what to expect, but felt, if she could get me to concentrate on something other than exhibitionism and playing the hooker, on something that brought my mind and body together, on some kind of connection to another person, I'd be relieved.

A week later Jahnet emailed back and gave me her phone number. She told me that, when she received my email, which I'd sent from work, she checked out my website, saw I worked in marketing and concluded we might be able to help each other out. I could help her advertise her new tantric life-coaching business; she could help me to explore the world of tantric. 'I'm taking classes and need six case studies in order to complete my course,' she said. 'Would you like to be one of them?' She explained it would mean having to commit an hour a week to come to her and study tantric. 'It'll be free for you.'

Being Jewish and a sucker for a bargain, I of course said yes. 'When can we start?' I typed.

Three weeks later I met Jahnet in her top-floor Maida Vale flat. I entered a large room filled with Shiva and Shakti statues, books on tantric and Eastern philosophies, and lots of Indian-patterned throw pillows. Large futons covered much of the floor, and a spiral staircase led up to the eaves. Incense scented the air and pale light came through the sheer orange curtains. I have not been to Bombay, but this seemed a close approximation.

She invited me to sit at a small round table in her lounge, then left to prepare a cup of mint tea. Tania had told me Jahnet was a tantric sex teacher. What she hadn't told me was that Jahnet was a sex worker as well, and had been in the profession for nearly thirty years. In combining the two specialities, Jahnet, I learnt, was the only tantric sex worker in the country.

'When I turned fifty-one,' she told me during that first meeting, 'I decided I was sick of working under the radar, and I wanted to do something more than just jerk guys off all day long.' She liked giving guys relief, she said, but wanted to add a more spiritual dimension to the act. Jahnet was an alluring half-Indian, half-English/Irish woman, large and voluptuous, with sizeable breasts and thick blonde streaks running through her dark shoulder-length hair. In a mature melodic voice, she told me about the course she was taking that she hoped would help legitimise her work. Jahnet had left school at sixteen, she explained, had no degree and very little discipline, but she was determined to take her career in a new direction while – remaining true to the spirit of a good sex worker – continuing to help others.

She was studying life coaching through the Open University. 'Darling, something in me believed there must be a way to harness all this sexual energy I was in contact with every day. I want to help people to achieve their goals – not just in sexual ways but in all aspects of their lives.' Just what I needed.

Our 'classes' were unusual and varied. We always started with a ceremonial bath. Jahnet would run the water while I undressed, fill the tub with flowers and scent, and then sponge me down. It got me in the mood for our sessions. It helped me to unwind, to the point where usually I wished I could just fall asleep; other times, it made me horny. But I had to remind myself I was there for neither of those things. Jahnet always wore a printed chiffon sarong, but had me sit naked on the futon, unless it was cold, and then I got a sarong of my own.

The first week the two of us practised breathing techniques, sitting cross-legged facing each other, our palms resting upwards on our laps. 'Take deep breaths while contracting your vagina,' Jahnet instructed. The idea was to understand and master my vaginal muscles, so, one day, like her, I could keep a man hard simply by flexing those muscles. She promised it would lead to better orgasms for me, too. Nothing wrong with that, I thought. I called this pussy aerobics. Like a workout session at the gym, it was exhausting. I left with an exhausted pussy that first day.

The second week Jahnet taught me the art of sensual massage by giving me a one-hour massage of my own. She climbed and writhed over my body while purring in my ear. Soon my entire being was vibrating from the sensation of being touched and stroked and caressed so lovingly. She explained the history of tantra, telling me how it originated in India some three thousand years ago. Tantric, she said, was a meditative form of sex where the object is to experience waves of pleasure, as opposed to a brief clitoral orgasm. A sensuous massage was one member of a whole family of pleasure. 'I can only teach you the basics,' she warned. 'You need to practise your vaginal contractions every day, remember. Once your muscles are tight, your orgasms will be deeper and longer.'

At the end of our third session, Jahnet gave me an orchid and instructed me to carry it with me until it fell apart. I put the flower in my handbag and took my handbag to work meetings, the gym, and then home. By the end of the day the petals were crushed and lay at the bottom of my bag. '"Orchid" means "testicles" in Greek,' said a friend when I told him about this exercise. I suspected there might be heavy meaning here but didn't dwell on it. I went back to my vaginal pumps.

Jahnet spent one session with her hand halfway up my vagina, instructing me in the finer points of vaginal- and anal-muscle control. She would put her fingers up my cunt to confirm I was contracting sufficiently. 'Squeeze tighter and hold!' she ordered. 'Squeeze!'

'This is exhausting,' I'd complain every week. 'It's not like my vagina muscles aren't in practice.'

'Yes, but it's not been the right kind of practice, my dear.' Jahnet was part scolding nanny, part sex instructor, part therapist. 'You're too much of an orgasm chaser, Suzanne darling. That's what your problem is.'

I supposed she had a point. Even Anthony, my hot cop, had said, the last time we met, 'You're smart and funny and great. Your biggest problem is that you let your pussy lead and your brain follow.'

Jahnet assured me that things would get better with time, that one day I'd see how tantra was about pleasure, not about coming.

'But how is this going to help me if my pussy's tired all the time?'

'All this swinging shit you've been doing has made you too fixated on coming, Suzanne,' she said. 'Just enjoy the pleasure. You need to relax, to let your mind connect with what's happening to your body, and to share your pleasure with your partner.' Tantric, she said, was about creating a circle of energy around me and my partner, the exact opposite of the solo fuckfest I'd been having in my brain in recent months.

One day Jahnet said something that really freaked me out: 'I don't want you to come until I see you next week. That's your homework.' Fortunately, she qualified it by saying I could masturbate but had to forget about coming. Once again she stressed that the goal was to stop me from being so completely orgasm-centric. Of course, I cheated. But I got to day four and thought that was pretty good for a beginner. And, when I came, it was fantastic.

I went through the entire course with Jahnet. At the end of our final session she set me my homework for the year. 'I want you to find three tantric lovers, men who you'll meet only for tantric and nothing else. No attachments.'

I said, 'Do you give this homework to all your students?'

'No,' she said. 'This homework is special to you. I don't think you need *one* man at the moment, like my other students; for you, I think three is about right.'

She explained how to approach my homework. 'You will put aside one or two weekends a month to see each one. In between, no contact. On the "tantric weekends" you will devote yourself exclusively to pleasure – of any kind, not just sexual.' Not seeing my partners too frequently, she said, would help me to keep the focus on the *act*, not the *man*. I suppose Jahnet thought that, if I transcended the emotional state, tantric would lead to a mind–body spirituality very unlike the body–body nonspirituality I was used to.

I liked the next part: 'On "tantric weekends" you must do absolutely nothing that is practical – no laundry, no cooking (unless you enjoy cooking) and no housekeeping. You should create a sacred space – away from the bedroom – to practise tantric sex, so that you are not limited by the confines of a bed and have space to move around in, to give each other massages, to play, to dance.'

Before I left, Jahnet told me that, when I found a tantric partner and if I wanted a little practice sesh, I should bring him with me and she would walk us through a tantric experience together. I thought it sounded a little kinky. Having someone watch me have sex with another person didn't sound much different from the swinging clubs.

'Where am I going to find these guys?' I asked her.

'That's for you to discover,' she said. 'I'm afraid I can't help you with that. It may take your meeting a dozen or more men before you find the three that are right for you.'

I thought the auditioning process could be fun.

I knew how to find a swinging partner but wasn't sure how to go about finding a tantric partner. I suspected that the Asda of dating sites, Match.com, would reject any ad from a woman looking for a tantric partner, interpreting 'tantric' as a code for soliciting. But, while looking around the internet, my standby pimp, I found a site called Tantra.com. Most of the men were in America. Still, I posted a personal.

What the fuck, it's free, I thought, and put an ad on SwingingHeaven as well. Subject heading: 'Can You Ride the Wave?'

Tantric student, 43, blonde, blue eyes, 5'5", seeks one or more tantric partners (not at the same time) who want to explore tantra but are not looking for a romantic relationship. Must be open to the idea that deep intimacy can exist outside of a monogamous love relationship.

I thought it would be worth a punt, even if it risked inundation by randy men attracted by the thought of six-hour sessions of no-strings-attached sex.

Within a couple of days I had fifty replies, mainly from the very men I feared my ad would attract. I didn't write to any of them. Soon after, my kids and I left for a three-week holiday in Vietnam. I figured I'd get my rest and relaxation, if not my tantric, there. I promised myself I'd practise the vaginal contractions and keep the masturbation to a minimum. And check the responses to my ads when I got back.

I brought to Vietnam a delicate jet choker that Jahnet gave me as a parting gift after our last session. 'When you see a large body of water on your trip,' she told me, 'I want you to throw it in and let it go.' So I did, my second day on the beach. I'd thought by then I'd gone through all the grieving I needed to do for Daniel. But, as I tossed the choker into the water, immediately I felt him pass through me. I had finally let him go.

When I returned to London, there was a message in an old hotmail address I no longer used. It was in response to a personal I'd placed on Match.com a year earlier and was from a guy named Jack.

12. A LITTLE LIKE FALLING IN LOVE

I'd posted my profile in a rage on Match.com a year earlier after yet another argument with Daniel over his smoking and drinking, and then forgot about it after we'd kissed and made up.

Jack's letter was intriguing. He explained that he'd been a private detective for twenty-seven years, had a house in west London and was looking for someone who enjoyed laughing, good food, clothes shopping and hot-weather holidays. At last, I thought, a man who rings my bells – has a job, has money, has similar interests. Ding, ding, ding. His picture showed a blondish middle-aged man with a well-worn face – a hot cross between David Bowie and Lance Henrikson. He was looking straight into the camera with an intense sexy stare. I thought he was one of the best-looking men I'd ever seen advertising on a website. His profile didn't say anything about tantric, but I was sufficiently inspired to feel I might entice him to give it a go.

I clicked Reply and up popped a form asking me to fill in the blanks and hand over £14.99. Fuck this, I thought. I'm not spending £14.99 to join Match just to meet one guy. It's my rule of thumb that, feminism aside, I don't pay for a first date – ironic, given I have no problem attracting impoverished guys happy to let me shell out from the second date on.

How many private dicks can there be in west London? I wondered. A quick Google search revealed all of one. I composed a note, then sat at my computer staring at the thing. I feared he might take me for a stalker, but soon concluded there wasn't too much at risk – if anything, I figured, as one who made his living snooping on others, he might actually respect the gesture – so hit Send and off went the note to his work email. I hoped he didn't have a PA who checked his inbox.

The next day I got my response. He'd been genuinely flattered that I'd gone out of my way to track him down, he said. He hinted at a past and said he was focusing on the future, was now looking to develop a one-on-one relationship with someone. I knew a relationship wasn't compatible with Jahnet's homework assignment to find three tantric lovers, but I thought perhaps I could bend the rules this one time. We arranged to meet in a week's time and in between spent hours on the phone talking about our jobs, our kids, our day. He had a west London accent and, as it turned out, was one of the rare residents of his trendy neighbourhood who had been born and bred there. His job sounded fascinating, a Raymond Chandler novel come to life, but Jack was more interested in talking about his sideline – counselling men on how to become more sensitive and caring and true to their inner tree-hugger. He'd take groups of men to the woods of Nowhere, where they'd have to rough it for a weekend – no showers, no shaving, no washing machine – and break down the macho walls through soul-searching questions. It sounded a bit new agey, a bit wanky, but I didn't want to say so.

When I told my colleague Louise about Jack one day at work, she said it for me. 'Beware guys who give counselling. It's usually because they are a fucked-up mess and need it themselves.' She suggested I stick to finding a nice normal simple guy who just wanted to take me out for a meal, buy me sweet little presents and have a real conversation with me from time to time. 'I'm not liking the sound of this new man, Suzanne.' She made finding a normal guy sound as easy as going to Waitrose for a pint of semi-skimmed.

On Saturday afternoon, four days before my scheduled date with Jack, fate intervened. I had taken my elder son, Alfred, to his favourite sports shop, Lillywhites, so he could blow his birthday money on the latest Arsenal jersey. The store was mad; the queue held twenty people and I was bored waiting. I gave Jack a ring. Turned out he was just around the corner, buying shirts on Jermyn Street. When my son heard me say, 'Oh, you're just around the corner from us!' he screamed, 'Can your friend pick us up, Mummy?'

It was not such a bad idea. We were loaded down with shopping, and schlepping our bags back on the Tube was a gruesome prospect. 'Would it be a big pain to come and get us?' I asked. As soon as the words were out, I remembered we'd not even met before. That's another catch about the cyber world: it gives a false sense of intimacy to people who aren't intimate – indeed, who don't even know each other – at all.

'No problem,' said Jack. 'I'll swing by in fifteen minutes.'

This isn't exactly what I had in mind for a first date, I thought. I was wearing turned-up jeans, a long brown sheepskin coat with a turquoise sweater underneath, no make-up and my hair was a mess.

We met in front of the Trocadero. A huge Volvo Estate pulled up to the pavement, complete with cream-coloured leather seats. 'Mum! Nice car!' said Alfred. We climbed in, me in the front seat, my son in the back. I took a look at Jack and saw he was just as handsome as he appeared in his picture. He was wearing a navy wool flat cap and a long blue overcoat. Stylish. Sexy.

'Well, this is an unusual first meeting,' I said, and introduced him to Alfred. 'Nice car, by the way. My son approves.'

'What she meant to say was that she's just glad you actually have a car. My mother doesn't usually go out with guys that drive. Isn't that right, Mum?' I was reminded of my first morning-after with Daniel, when Alfred had told Daniel my farts smelt really bad.

'Yes, that's true,' I had to admit. 'Thanks for that, honey. It's great going on a first date with you.' Too bad there isn't a zipper I could pull so I could close his mouth every time he meets one of my new boyfriends, I thought.

We made small talk on the way. 'So, you're into sports, huh?' said Jack to Alfred. 'What team do you support?'

'Arsenal.'

'Good team. A friend of mine has season tickets.' He thought for a moment. 'Maybe I'll see if he ever has a spare.'

Good sign, I thought. Ingratiate yourself with the kid to get through to the mum. Excellent.

When we arrived back at the house, Alfred said, 'He's really cool. You are going to go out with him, aren't you?' Then, yelling to his younger brother, he said, 'Hey, Martin, Mum's actually met a cool guy with a nice car!'

The attraction between us had been instantaneous. He smiled at me and I smiled back – not the *oh-shit!* smile but the *oooh, all right!* smile. He called me as soon as he got home and said, 'Are you free tonight?'

We met up at the Electric, a members-only bar on Portobello Road a short walk from his house. Jack didn't drink, didn't smoke, didn't take drugs, I learnt. The history he'd alluded to was a long tale of substance-abuse problems. Sounds like a lot of the guys I've dated, I thought, as he gave me the synopsis. Jack assured me that for him it really was history, not, as was the case with Daniel and some others, history in the making. He hadn't touched drink or drugs in twenty years, he said, not since learning he'd contracted all three forms of hepatitis. He led an ultra-clean life now, stuck to a very strict diet – no sugar, no fats – and, following the year of hellish treatments that successfully got rid of the hepatitis, become something of a monk – well, a monk that fucked.

I'd met guys before who didn't drink or smoke or take drugs. But usually they hadn't dropped all three. If they'd given up one, typically they stuck passionately to the other two, substituting one addiction only to focus on another. If their new vice wasn't in the top three, then usually it was sex.

Within two hours of our first one-on-one meeting, we were back at Jack's place, where he gave me a guided tour of his house that ended in the bedroom.

I stood in the doorway and pulled out a line from my personal inventory. 'Don't you think it's time to kiss me?' He did think it was time to kiss me, and more. Being a 'new man', Jack didn't do the fuck-'n'-go. He didn't do quickies at all, in fact. With him, sex was like a five-course meal or a very long symphony – or tantric, for that matter. He took things slowly.

That first evening was like many that followed. Once I got into bed with him, it would be three hours before I got out of it. Jahnet would be proud of me, I thought. Sex with Jack was just like she'd taught me it should be. I felt very close to my new lover. I got into the rhythm and pleasure, the intimacy of being with him. And Jack just wanted to be with me. His bedroom was a world away from the swinging clubs and sex parties. When we made love, Jack was sensuous, and I felt my whole body respond to his.

Except I couldn't come.

I put it down to nerves. This guy was ringing all my other bells, and perhaps I was scared. It was easy to come when I didn't give a shit, but here was a contender, a man with whom I felt a real connection, and I didn't want to fuck it up.

We both jumped into the relationship with our feet pressed firmly on the accelerator. 'I'd like a completely honest monogamous relationship,' he said that first night, explaining that he couldn't be intimate with more than one person at a time. 'I'm looking for something deeply committed.' Jack knew that I liked swinging, but admitted he wouldn't have been able to handle my carrying on with other guys, even if I were honest and upfront about it.

I promised to give it up. 'I'm bored with it anyway,' I said, both to him and to myself. I spent the next two days texting all the men in my phonebook. My fingers did twitch a bit as I sent the message to some of my favourite funboys. Still, the message was the same, and to the point: HI. I'VE MET SOMEONE. I WON'T BE AVAILABLE ANY MORE. TAKE CARE. SUZANNE. Sometimes before hitting Send I'd wonder if perhaps it was a bit premature to be agreeing to settle down, but I figured I could always pick up the habit again without too much bother. Send. Send. Send.

My swinging partner, Greg, texted back. WELL, HE MUST BE SOME GUY IF HE'S GOT YOU TO GIVE UP SWINGING. ARE YOU SURE YOU CAN HANDLE BEING WITH JUST ONE MAN? I DON'T REALLY SEE YOU AS THE RELATIONSHIP TYPE.

I did.

On day two, after another three-hour fuck session, Jack looked into my eyes as I was leaving and said, 'I asked the universe for what I wanted and it brought me you.'

I'm really a sucker for lines like that. He looked like he believed it. My friends, however, looked like they thought I was nuts when I told them what Jack had said.

'Take it slow,' said my friend, Pat. 'You don't want to be seeing so much of him so early on in the relationship.'

'I know, but he's great. Really.'

'You'll be burnt out before you know it,' she warned. 'He's fresh out of a relationship, so take it slow.'

On day three Jack rang me up and said, 'Look, I know we've only just met and it's probably too soon to be doing stuff like this, but would you and the boys like to come with me and my daughter on a holiday to Brazil in six weeks' time?' As I caught my breath, he rushed on. 'All expenses paid. It's just that, if I don't book the flight now, they'll be sold out.'

'Sounds fabulous,' I said in bed later that day after another bedroom marathon.

On day four, another three hours of fucking. 'You know, I was thinking,' said Jack, 'wouldn't it be great if you could buy the house just next door so we could spend more time together without actually living together?'

As I drove home, Bernadette rang. 'Where were you last night? I tried to ring you.'

'I was with Jack.'

'Weren't you with Jack the night before, too?'

'Yup. And the night before that, too.'

'Be careful,' she warned. 'So many nights in a row and you've only just met. Sounds obsessive to me.'

Day five Jack sent a huge bouquet of flowers to my office. The night before, he had told me I had bad breath; this was his atonement. Louise looked at the flowers and rolled her eyes. 'Watch out for the therapists.'

The flowers were magnificent but, as I'd never been told I had bad breath before, I had become obsessed well before their arrival. Perhaps in an effort to take the edge off my obvious discomfort, Jack had theorised that my gut might be the culprit – irritable bowel syndrome, perhaps – thus nudging the issue out of the grooming and into the medical realm. I booked a colonic irrigation. I changed my diet, removing apples and broccoli and garlic from the menu. I bought acidophilus tablets to balance the pH of my stomach. I was permanently on edge, trying to smell my own breath and making sure I had a pack of Orbit Professional in my handbag at all times.

Still, by day seven I was head over heels. And Jack's seven-year-old daughter was in love with me, as I had two boys she could pretend were her big brothers, while in me a new shopping companion.

Jack believed I was 'the one'. And, as he rang so many of my bells, I was happy to be his one and only. He bought me a chocolate knee-length corduroy skirt when we went shopping in Portobello; he took me for oysters at Bibendum; he sent me loving text messages (CAN'T WAIT TO SLIP MYSELF INSIDE YOU!) and bouquets of flowers with sweet notes attached (*I choose* you!). One day, while walking through Portobello, he said, 'I think you're a girl who really needs to be treated well, and that's what I want to do. I really want to make you feel special.' I did feel special.

Except, sometimes, in bed. I had my doubts we were truly compatible. Sex was problematic, or rather, having an orgasm was. I didn't come until day six and, though that might seem speed of light among women who come once a year, I've always been able to come in a flash, from the first date. Days one, two, three, four and five, I tried every position from the *Kama Sutra* and nothing worked. Dutifully, I followed Jahnet's advice and tried to focus on the pleasure, and, while making love with Jack was very pleasurable indeed, by our third session I just wanted to get there, the tantric way or any other.

So I had three problems. One, I couldn't come. Two, I'm a size queen. Three, I couldn't tell a man whose penis was the national average that average didn't work for me.

Jack tried to compensate by going down on me, but sometimes a girl can sense if a guy's heart really isn't in it. I didn't know how to climax without pushing the usual fantasy buttons in my brain. Physically, we just didn't fit together. Finally, feeling unbelievably frustrated, I found a way to orgasm. It was called pornography. Our sixth time together, during another three-hour sesh, my heart and body were feeling fine but I knew that once again I wasn't going to come.

'Do you have any pornography?' I asked.

'Yeah, sure. What do you like?'

'Gang bangs, double penetration, anal – that sort of thing.'

Jack got up, put on a tape and fast-forwarded to a scene featuring two couples swapping and then the two guys doing one of the girls. I sat on Jack's face, facing the TV. Three minutes later I came. I was embarrassed. 'I'm really sorry,' I said.

'Don't be. I want to do whatever it takes to make you happy.'

'I know, Jack. But I wanted to stop watching porn. I wanted to stop getting off on gang bangs and all that shit. I just wanted to see if I could be intimate with you.'

The test of any relationship is usually a holiday, and we were on the motherfucker of all holidays, a hastily arranged trip to Bahrain we took six weeks after we met.

I'd talked Jack out of the holiday in Brazil after he told me the place he had in mind was quite remote, two days from London, and involved every form of transport, including feet, to get to. He'd been a couple of times before and wanted to show me his dream place.

'It's an idyllic beach resort, Suzanne,' he said. 'Secluded, romantic and cheap.'

'Yes, it does sound great – for a three-week break,' I said. 'But we've only got one week. Once we factor in the four days travelling, we've got only three days in paradise. And then there's the jet lag.' I suggested we go somewhere easier and closer to home.

As he had booked another inspirational tree-hugging week for himself and was leaving for the California desert in a couple of days, Jack had little time to find an alternative for us. It was now three weeks after our initial discussion about a holiday together, and just three weeks to half-term. 'Why don't you call my brother-in-law?' he suggested. 'He's an ex-airline pilot. He's always coming up with cheap flights to exotic destinations.'

'Has your brother-in-law heard of half-term?' I said. So close to the student holiday, when half of England is on an aeroplane, I knew any place exotic was going to be booked up and the only holiday destinations still available would be the ones no one else wanted. Hence Brazil became Dubai, and at an exorbitant price.

Then the brother-in-law rang to say he couldn't find us a hotel room. We settled on Bahrain, the only alternative presented. I didn't know much about the Gulf and, though it didn't sound as desirable as Brazil, I wasn't paying and was still loved up, and thought, How bad can it be? All the photos I'd ever seen of the place were desert shots, and to me desert equalled hot. The Hawar Resort's online brochure described a state-of-the-art hotel on its own sandy beach, with the usual luxury facilities, plus three restaurants – all at the bargain price of £50 per room per night. Kids were free and so was the food.

Being Jewish, once again I thought I'd scored the biggest bargain in the world. Jack's going to be so proud of me, I thought, as I've saved him so much money. The idea of spending seven glorious days on the beach, six glorious nights shagging this man's brain's out – how could I not find a way to come? It all sounded so splendid.

We had to spend the first night in downtown Bahrain, as the boats to our beach paradise didn't leave till the next morning. As we checked into our hotel we passed a Wild West-themed bar full of American guys who worked on oil rigs, who'd come for an alcohol-fuelled weekend break and who I soon discovered got louder by the hour. We stayed in our rooms and watched satellite television.

'Don't worry, kids,' I said. 'There's beach buggies and table tennis and paddle boats and jetskis at the resort.' And room service and a gift shop and a mini bar for us, I thought, looking ahead.

The next day, a minibus picked us up and drove an hour to the jetty, where we waited with a half-dozen other people. That should have been a warning right there. No other kids, just three Arab guys who didn't look at us and two women wearing burkhas.

'Are we just the leftovers?' I whispered to Jack. 'I hope the other children are already there.'

He shrugged.

Approaching the island, we saw a vast white monstrosity looming over the beach in isolation. No other buildings.

As we exited the speedboat, I saw that the beach was empty, and then saw why. The sand was black and dirty and littered with rubbish, the water a murky colour that didn't look safe to swim in. Not that we'd want to. I bent over and put my hand in and it was surprisingly cold.

At least there were jetskis lined up on the shore, and I saw a large swimming pool, a seaside restaurant and a beach-buggy track. The only thing missing was people.

'Are there other people coming?' I asked the man standing at the reception desk.

'Tomorrow,' he said. 'All coming tomorrow. Lots of people. Hotel almost full.'

We weren't convinced. '*The Shining* could have been filmed in this place,' said Jack under his breath. Over the course of our stay we saw only a handful of people, none of whom looked particularly fun to hang out with.

Suddenly I remembered I was in a Muslim country. The only staff were men, all dark-haired with moustaches and unstylish haircuts, and all staring at pasty blonde me when they didn't think I was looking, as if I were the first Western woman they'd seen in a very long time. They were awkward and uncomfortable in my presence and didn't quite know how to behave towards me. I let Jack do all the talking.

'Where's the restaurant?' he enquired.

'Only one restaurant open. Rest closed,' said a man with a moustache and unstylish haircut. He pointed to a place that looked more like a café. 'Over there.'

The food looked like leftovers from the British Airways flight we took to get there. It came out in large metal trays and had obviously been preheated, not prepared specially for us. The centre of each tray was cold and the outer edge of the dish merely warm.

But eating was as fun as it got there, at least until the fourth day, when we stopped doing even that. The country was suffering from a rare cold spell. I had expected twenty-seven degrees; it was closer to seven. I wore my sexy dresses – each earmarked for its own special day – all at once, one over the other. The layered look. I felt camouflaged like the burkha babes I'd seen on the jetty, who'd then disappeared.

I didn't get the sense that other guests had disappeared. I got the sense none ever existed.

'Tomorrow,' said the concierge each time we asked. 'All coming tomorrow. Lots of people. Hotel almost full.'

'Mum, what are we expected to do now?' Alfred and Martin asked by the hour. 'There's no kids here, Mummmmm. There's nothing to dooooooooooo.'

The unheated pool was too cold, but the kids did put on a couple of sweaters and jetskied two or three times until the thrill was gone. Mostly, we played endless rounds of table tennis.

Jack and I tried to make the best of what was obviously a really bad situation. I couldn't help thinking back to my first holiday with David and how, had he been here, he would have handled it. 'When we get back to London, I want you to demand a full refund for this holiday,' I could picture him saying. 'Where the fuck did you find this place, anyway?'

On day four, Valentine's Day, Jack said, 'I can't take it any more. I can't eat the food one more day. This is my first proper holiday in four years.'

That was news to me. I felt even worse than I'd been feeling from the day we arrived, and that was saying something.

'I want to eat good food in a nice hotel,' he continued. 'I want to be with people who are wearing something other than tracksuits and burkhas. I want to swim in a warm pool. I want to sleep on Egyptian-cotton sheets. We've got to get out of here.'

'If only,' I said. 'Perhaps we can nick the jetskis and escape off the island.'

Jack wasn't laughing. 'I've got an idea!' he said suddenly, his eyes staring into the distance. 'Why don't you ring up the Ritz Carlton in Bahrain? Say you're organising a conference there for next year and want to check out the hotel as a possible venue – and by the way, you're travelling with your family. Might they give any sort of discount off the rack rate?'

Sounded fabulous, except for the part about making it all happen. 'I don't see why you can't do it yourself,' I said. 'You are, after all, a private detective. You make a living out of getting stuff out of people.'

'Mostly information,' he said. He thought a lie might work better coming from a woman. I did as I was told, and miraculously the conference manager bought the story. We got two nights, discounted 75 per cent. Suzanne saves the day, I thought. Hurrah!

The Ritz was a five-star dream. We found our paradise at last. We got the Egyptian-cotton sheets, the heated pool, the gorgeous food.

But it was not enough to save the relationship. Shortly after we returned to London, Jack took off for the Midlands for another inspirational tree-hugging weekend. When he didn't call me on the drive back home, as he usually did, I became concerned. It had been snowing hard that day and the snow had stuck and turned to ice, something rare for England. The radio stations broadcast travel advisories. I rang his mobile and the call went straight to his answering machine. I rang his home and it did the same. I went to bed feeling anxious and upset. The next day, I tried his office and got him.

'What happened to you?' I said. 'I thought I was going to hear from you last night. I tried to ring you and there was no answer.'

'I'm sorry,' he said. 'I was on the phone to Stephanie for three hours.' Stephanie was the ex. This was the first time Jack had mentioned speaking to her since I'd met him. He had assured me their break-up had been final, and I believed him, given she'd punched him and fractured one of his ribs the last time they'd been together. Sounded pretty final to me. 'She rang me up and we stayed up talking. She said some things that wound me up and really touched a nerve. I should have called you up, though. Sorry.'

After that call, Jack became more and more distant.

Two weeks later, I called him on it. 'What's going on? You don't ring me like you used to. You don't touch me any more. We haven't had sex in weeks. You seem distant.'

I half-hoped I'd hear reassurances, but I knew I was on the way out.

'I don't find you sexually attractive any more,' he said.

I was stunned. I wasn't expecting that exit line. 'I don't get it. You were all over me like a rash just a few weeks ago,' I said. 'Now you're completely turned off? I haven't changed. I haven't done anything different from usual.'

He didn't answer. I was puzzled. I'd always been told I was sexy. Now I was being told I wasn't sexy enough. I'd dumped my swinging partners, ignored Jahnet's homework of finding three tantric partners and settled on one, all for a few nice treats and some good but unfulfilling sex. Maybe he just didn't want to say what we both knew: we didn't fit.

I was rebound girl, just as Pat had predicted. Jack had broken up with his previous girlfriend only six weeks before we met. Now the warning signs I'd so happily ignored flashed into my brain, and I pictured the night we lay in bed after fucking, my head on his chest, when I'd asked Jack when he'd last had a relationship.

'It ended six weeks ago, when she punched me after I said something she didn't like,' he said.

Bitch, I thought – as opposed to what in retrospect would have been the more-reasonable response: Danger! Fresh wound!

'She cracked one of my ribs,' he continued, 'and I told her to go. And that was the end of that.'

'Wow, she must have been really pissed off,' I said.

'Yes, she was. But it wasn't going to work anyway. She wanted kids and I don't want any more.' Jack was very convincing, and I believed he had convinced himself. 'She loves getting drunk and I don't drink. Even when I looked at pictures of the two of us together, I just thought, "We *so* don't fit".'

'Mmmn,' I said. 'Six weeks? That's not a very long time. Are you sure I'm not rebound girl?' I laughed, lightening the mood and hopping right over the obvious bump in our road.

'Rebound girl?' he said. 'Oh, don't be silly, honey. I love you.'

The night he broke up with me, Jack said my desire to have sex all the time while we were on holiday showed him how needy I was. He didn't do needy, he said. This, too, came as a surprise. Stuck in our sandpit oblivion that grim week, my only need was for a diversion. Nothing to do, nowhere to go, nothing to eat. Nothing to do but fuck. Even though we had got along, had made the best of things, and even laughed at the ridiculousness of our situation, something had turned off in Jack's brain and I hadn't noticed.

I had thought we were OK. Indeed, on the plane back to London Jack had taken my hand and, under the aeroplane blanket, put my hand on his lap, inviting a hand-job through his trousers. As I felt his cock get hard I looked across the aisle at our kids, all asleep. Everything's OK, I thought. If we could endure seven days together in a Gulf hell, we could endure anything.

'I'm sorry it didn't work out, dear,' my mother said when I called with the news. 'Maybe the next time you get involved with someone, you should get a reference from two ex-girlfriends.'

If Jack didn't do needy, I didn't do break-ups. I tend to recompartmentalise. I liked the guy. Hell, he was one of the few men in my life who was a self-made success story and who had a car and a house of his own. He was a grown-up. And, despite his 'new man' ramblings, he was fun to be around.

Plus, I didn't know any other straight men who wanted to watch *Nip/Tuck* with me. We remained friends. Within two weeks he was back with Stephanie, and within two days I was back at Rio's, in the red room, with a tall black man with a big black cock.

13. HOMEWORK

Fucking a black guy with a big black cock wasn't the magic salve I'd hoped it would be. Being rejected hurt, and an afternoon at Rio's, though fun, wasn't a cure-all for being dumped.

The next day I rang up Jahnet. I told her about Jack and how he'd given me my walking papers. I told her how sad I felt, how disappointed.

She wasn't particularly sympathetic. 'I want you to come over here and see me. Now!' Her tone reminded me of the way I spoke with my boys when they'd misbehaved.

Within a half-hour I was sitting naked on a futon in her apartment.

'I explained your homework,' she said. 'No boyfriends. Three tantric partners. You're not ready for a relationship, Suzanne.'

I had thought I was. But I knew now she was right. As were my many friends who had warned me not to jump in so fast. I should have stuck to my homework.

'Let out the loudest scream you can,' Jahnet instructed. 'I want you to scream as if your life depended on it and, as you do, I want you to think about getting that man out of your system.'

I screamed so loudly I thought someone might call the cops.

'Now,' said my tantric-sex teacher, satisfied, 'I want you to start on your homework. *Again*.'

I went back to my PC and signed onto SwingingHeaven. The ad I'd placed just before leaving for Vietnam and meeting Jack had attracted another twenty-five responses. Unfortunately, just like with the previous sixty, the men in my inbox fancied marathon sex sessions and expressed no interest in the spiritual side. I didn't like the look of any of them either. So I put an ad on JDate, a website for Jews wanting to meet other Jews. Maybe a nice Jewish boy, for a change, I thought. I hadn't been on a date with one of my own since I'd met David, and even that had been a fluke.

'So,' I said to David as we lay in bed one morning a few days after we first had sex, 'what's your religion?'

'You're kidding me, right?'

'No,' I said. I hadn't a clue. 'You look Italian or Spanish, maybe.' I always ended up with naughty Catholic boys, so assumed he was one, too.

'I'm Jewish,' he said. 'Mother's Jewish, father's Jewish. I'm one hundred per cent Jew.'

'You're kidding, right?' I said. 'You're *Jewish*?'

'Is that so weird?' he said, starting to look annoyed.

'I never meet Jews,' I said. 'Like, never.' My mother is going to love you, I thought.

Even though the marriage didn't work out, the Jewish connection did. I can't quite say what makes a Jew different from anyone else. All I know is that, when I meet a fellow Jew, I know it – David being the one exception of a lifetime. Maybe it's the humour, the way of looking at the world, the work ethic or the fact that, deep down, we bond, knowing we're not the world's favourite people. Whatever the cause, after finding out that David was Jewish too, I felt a connection to him that had been absent with other men.

As I filled in the blanks on my JDate profile, I wrote nothing about my quest for a tantric partner. That, I figured, I could reveal later and, given that JDate was a 'straight' site and not a swinging one, I didn't want anyone thinking I was soliciting. A year earlier, while filling out my profile on TotallyGorgeous.com, I'd put 'big cocks' next to the question 'What do you like?' A month later I was barred. 'Dear Suzanne,' said my reject letter. 'We have terminated your membership, as we've noticed you're using it inappropriately. Our site promotes relationships, not sex.' Funny, I'd thought at the time, as why else would someone go on a dating site? 'I hadn't realised modern relationships no longer involved sex,' I wrote back.

Nonetheless, I'd learnt my lesson: no mention of big cocks and no mention of tantric partners either.

Julius sounded like the best prospect of the lot. The rest were a bunch of desperate-looking Jewish men, most of whom seemed to have been recently divorced. I refused to play the rebound girl again.

We had a brief chat on the phone. He told me he was an entrepreneur who had run a music-booking agency and then started a music magazine. After selling the magazine he didn't have to work very hard any more, so now he 'dabbled', he said, in internet businesses. I found that meant he owned a couple of dating sites, plus a shopping site, and a few other operations besides. Then he got down to business.

'Are you a dominatrix?' he asked out of the blue. 'How do you feel about caning?'

'Me or you?' I asked.

He told me he thought it would be saucy if I whacked his butt a few strokes.

'Well,' I said, 'it would be something new.'

He sounded nice enough, for a masochist. And he said he looked like Andy Garcia. He hadn't posted a picture to prove it, but I took his word for it and arranged to meet him at an Italian restaurant not far from his home in Maida Vale. I've always had a thing for Andy Garcia, who for a number of years had popped up in my dreams with such disturbing regularity it felt like I was cheating on my husband.

When I got to the restaurant, I spotted Julius standing by the bar. He was smoking – a bad sign, though after Daniel I'd tried to relax my view on that and had reached a kind of compromise, I'd fuck a man who smoked but I wouldn't go out with him. As I walked towards Julius, I started calculating his chances. He may have fancied himself an Andy Garcia type, but the only resemblance I could make out was that both were Mediterranean looking. I had always assumed Andy Garcia, like all movie stars, was, if not larger than life, at least tall. Julius didn't top 5'8". Average height, average weight, above-average nose, above-average hair loss. He was about fifty and, though not unattractive, he was no movie star.

We had a nice meal together. With business contacts in common, we found enough to talk about without lapsing into embarrassing pauses over our rocket salads and pizza. Julius wasn't dull, but I suspected he wasn't exciting enough to spend an entire weekend with either. After a couple of glasses of wine, I started feeling tipsy and a little horny too. I looked over at my dinner companion and wondered what he would be like in bed.

Thinking about Jahnet's homework, I realised it would be a tremendous challenge to find *any* man I could be intimate with for an entire weekend. Aside from Jack, Daniel and Frank, I hadn't spent a full weekend with anyone since being married, and even my married years barely counted. Most weekends, David went to the office while I took the kids to the playground or out shopping. Tantric or no tantric, I thought, it's going to have to be one special man who I can stand for forty-eight hours.

'Should we have a nightcap back at my place?' Julius said, as the waitress cleared our plates. 'It's just around the corner.'

What the hell, I thought. 'Sure,' I said.

Walking into Julius's one-bedroom flat near the Regent's Canal, I noticed two things: one, he had a hell of a lot of locks on his door; two, the place was unbelievably tidy. His books were arranged in size order. He had white sofas that were still white. There was no paper in sight. I've always been wary of superclean guys, having put in my time married to one. I know the likelihood they spend their holidays vacuuming is, like, 500:1. As for the locks on the door, they freaked me out. I didn't see anything particularly priceless as I looked around the flat. Maybe there's something buried under the floorboards, I thought. Or *someone*. I stuck around anyway.

'Should we get started?' I suggested. 'I must warn you, I've never used a cane before.'

That didn't seem to bother Julius. He took a tie out of his wardrobe and asked me to bind him to the wardrobe handles, a foot above my head. 'Please,' he begged.

I graciously complied, wrapping his wrists together and then suspending him as requested. He remained fully clothed, tied to the wardrobe with his chest against the doors. I assumed he hadn't wanted to take his clothes off because he was worried I might hurt him too much. But then I thought, Surely that's the point?

The bedroom was small, giving me only a couple of feet between the bottom of the double bed and the wardrobe. 'The cane is in the bottom drawer of the side cabinet by the bed,' he said. 'Can you get it out? Please?'

I grabbed the cane. It looked just like the ones headmasters use on naughty boys in movies about boarding schools. At last, my Hollywood moment, I thought. Get ready, Andy Garcia.

I said, 'I think this would be a lot better if you dropped your trousers, don't you?'

'Yes, probably a good idea.'

I unzipped his jeans and pulled them down, along with his black Calvin Klein underwear. His ass was round and hairy. I struck him with the cane. It was surprisingly easy to use and, after a few whacks, Julius's ass was a pleasant shade of pink and he had an erection.

'This is fun,' I said. 'I haven't whipped anyone since a girl passed me her cat-o'-nine-tails at Rudegirls, an all-girl club I go to from time to time. She pulled down her leopard-print skirt to reveal the most perfect black ass and I whipped her while she bent over a table. That was horny.' I cracked the cane twice more across his ass.

'Sounds it,' he said, more interested in his own pain than in hearing about someone else's. 'Would you hit me a few more times? Please?'

'I don't know if I should,' I teased. 'I might want you to fuck me first. Or maybe I should just leave you tied up there for a while.'

'Please. Hit me.'

'I'm enjoying this, Julius. Making you wait.' I did rather dig the role-playing. Perhaps I could be a dominatrix after all, I thought.

'Please.'

'Oh, all right,' I said. *Crack. Crack. Crack.*

'That's enough. Thank you.'

I was tempted to give him another crack, just to show him who was boss. 'No problem,' I said instead. I untied Julius's hands. 'Now would you like to fuck me? You look ready.'

He was ready.

'Do you have any condoms?' I asked.

'Condoms?' He sounded surprised. 'No, I don't.'

'What, no condoms? Don't you ever have sex?'

'To be honest, I haven't had sex in ages,' he said. 'I'm sorry. I guess I should have been more prepared.'

I was. I ran out to my car and got my kitbag.

Back at the flat, Julius had turned off the lights and lit a couple of candles. I wasn't feeling particularly romantic after the caning. I was feeling powerful, though. I really wanted to use this guy now. It seemed inappropriate to turn submissive after having just caned his ass. If I were going to be his fantasy, he could be mine. I wanted to remain the one in control.

I sucked his cock to make him hard again, put a condom on him and straddled him, grinding down on his cock. 'Do you like being fucked like this? Did you enjoy being whipped?'

'Yes,' he whimpered. 'I enjoyed it – very, very much indeed.'

'Would you like me to stick a butt plug up my ass while you fuck me?'

'Do you *like* that?' He looked shocked. I thought that pretty funny, coming from someone who'd just begged to be caned.

'Of course I like it,' I said, and grabbed the four-inch ribbed butt plug from my bag. I greased the plug with some lube, also from my bag, and then glided it up my ass.

'Why don't you fuck me from behind,' I suggested. 'It's a better view.'

'You're the wildest woman I've ever met!' he said. 'I'm going to come!' And he did.

I didn't.

'I better get home,' I said. 'I've got to pick my kids up early tomorrow.'

I put on my clothes while Julius unlocked the many locks on his door. I was home in ten minutes. I walked straight upstairs to my computer, logged on to JDate and suspended my account. That's enough of Jewish men for a while, I thought.

The next morning I checked my email and found a message alert in the inbox. Someone from Tantra.com had responded to my ad. I signed on, for the hell of it, though all the responses I'd had to date had come from men living in the US. After Frank, I'd steered clear of even corresponding with anyone living on the other side of the pond. Sure enough: an American, this one a guy living in the Catskills. Not another New Yorker, I thought, disappointed, and as I moved my cursor towards Delete a picture loaded in the corner of the screen. An arty shot, in sepia tone, showing a very slim man with wavy shoulder-length hair and a huge smile. He was wearing a pair of large sunglasses and no shirt, just a towel wrapped around his shoulders. He was holding a canoe paddle. 'Musician and healer,' said his profile. A sexy hippy, seemed to me.

Hi there, tantric student. Hmmm. Yes, I can ride the wave for hours – it is such delight, eh? I live in a beautiful home in the mountains north of NYC and am also looking for tantric partners. Do you ever come to the USA? Much peace to you!

It did seem somewhat idiotic to respond but, then, he was cute. And I did go to New York from time to time. And he did practise tantric. I could probably arrange to meet him a couple of times a year, I figured. Jahnet never said my partner had to live in the UK.

So I wrote back. I discovered we had a great deal in common, so much so that it was odd our paths had not crossed before. Scott was friends with a musician who'd played in a famous 60s band my uncle was in. And he'd later played bass for a notorious 80s group whose lead singer was now in another band being produced by one of my clients. His only London friend – like Scott, a massage therapist – was a man who had known Jahnet for twenty-three years.

Goodie! I thought. Another tantric connection. All we needed was to find ourselves on the same continent sometime. Why is it that all the good ones always seem to live on the other side of the world?

Meanwhile, I scheduled a few more dates with local guys, for homework. With the tantric not really panning out, I put another ad on SwingingHeaven, omitting all tantric references and, in a nod to my original ad, stipulating Radio 4 listeners only, and for once my timing was spot on. Trawling through the hundred-plus emails I received back, I located a handful of professional good-looking guys. Suddenly, I seemed to be on a roll. I was hopeful of finding someone who'd be hip to being an occasional tantric partner.

Omar was one. He said he worked at a film-production company, played tennis regularly and liked going to art galleries, the theatre and concerts. And he listened to Radio 4 regularly. 'To me, going out on a Sunday afternoon for an excellent meal and a glass of the old Chablis on the Embankment is my idea of bliss,' he wrote. 'Sharing the bottle with you would be very decent indeed.'

He sounded lovely. But it was the pictures he enclosed that really caught my eye. He sent three: the first, of his face, wasn't bad: short hair, full lips, large brown eyes, high cheekbones. Then a shot of his cock, soft. Impressive. The third also featured his cock, this time hard, and next to a twelve-inch ruler. The cock was longer.

'Nice cock. Are you free on Friday night?' I wrote, giving him my mobile number. He wrote back the next day and invited me to a movie. I'm not meeting a man, I thought. I'm meeting a cock.

I met him at the Swiss Centre in Leicester Square. Omar looked just like his photo, the clothed photo, anyway – always a pleasant surprise, considering how many vintage pix people post, pre-bald, pre-fat, pre-wrinkles, pre-1995. He was black, about six feet tall and very slim, with short hair and a big smile. He was wearing jeans, a striped shirt and black, square-toed loafers. He looked as relaxed as any man with a foot-long cock would. He saw me and smiled.

We kissed hello and then he let out a bizarre laugh – high, almost a giggle, almost feminine. Not a turn-on, but then I was looking for a tantric partner, not a full-time boyfriend, and, given the choice, a good cock beats a bad laugh.

'Follow me,' I said after the movie. 'I have a bottle of wine at my place. Interested?'

He was, and got in the car. On the way back to mine he said, 'So, what do you have in mind?'

'A bath,' I said. 'I'm thinking about taking a bath with you. I'm thinking a nice hot bath would be the perfect way to start off the evening. With a joint.'

'I've never started with a bath,' said Omar.

'It's a tantric thing,' I explained. 'Cleansing, relaxing.'

'Tantric, huh?' Omar arched one eyebrow alluringly. 'Tell me more.'

I told him about my lessons and my homework assignment. 'I could certainly be up for that,' he said.

Half an hour later we were in my house, smoking a joint and lying naked in my big bathtub. The water was hot and scented with rose oil. The only light came from two candles, just enough that I could see an extremely impressive cock floating to the surface. Huge, as advertised. It was like a baby's arm. And then it got bigger. I got wet just looking at it.

Stretching my toes towards him, I played with it, rubbing my feet up and down the shaft. I wondered how much blood it took to get a cock like that hard. I wondered if he passed out when he came or even before he got there, given how much blood and energy must have gone into making that thing work.

That huge diversion aside, the bath was relaxing, if a little cramped, and we stayed in the water until it grew cool. Omar didn't seem to be in a rush, so he'd passed the first tantric test. 'It's all about taking your time. There is no rush,' Jahnet had told me. We each grabbed a towel, dried off and went to my 6'6" super-king-size bed, a bed made for sex. I can do anything on that bed, and have – change positions three times without falling over the side, or sleep with a stranger and forget he's there. When my husband-to-be and I bought the bed, some fifteen years earlier, the sales assistant told us it was a great bed for starting a family. He should have said, 'This is a bed built for sex,' because that's what it became, especially after the divorce.

Omar was very slim, but had an athlete's body and impressive muscle definition – a well-defined six-pack, solid pecs, meaty biceps. But that wasn't what I was thinking about. I was thinking about what he was going to feel like in my mouth and inside of me. I did not have to wait too long to find out.

I got on my knees and went between his legs, holding his heavy cock in my hands, almost distracted by my newly red-lacquered fingernails, tarted up just for our date. But not so distracted. He was very hard and very thick. I put him in my mouth and could just about take in the head. I could tease him, but there was no chance of deep throating. So I thought of Jahnet's advice: 'Relax, darling. Learn to relax, take your time.' I relaxed the muscles of my jaw, and the technique seemed to work.

'Oh, God,' he said. 'That's unbelievably good.' We reversed positions so that we were lying side by side but with our heads on opposite ends of the bed, his cock in my mouth, his tongue in my pussy. I was very wet.

I loved fucking Omar. He proved the lyrics to the Maria Muldaur song 'it ain't the meat, it's the motion' are bullshit. It *is* the meat; a big cock inside a tight pussy is a fantastic feeling. Omar and I fucked and fucked and fucked that evening. He had incredible stamina. This guy doesn't know squat about tantric sex, I thought, but he sure knows plenty about self-control. I thought of how I'd fallen off the tantric wagon, and how someone like Omar might get me back on.

I didn't think about coming, and it took all my tantric powers not to. Just picturing Omar's huge cock made me swoon. But I knew my history: once I come, I want to go – it's over. In that sense, I'm a bit like a man. After coming, I want to roll over and go to sleep. The catch is, if my partner hasn't come by the time I have, I'm stuck waiting it out, lying back and thinking of England.

'Would you like to fuck me up the ass?' I said to Omar. I thought that might get him to shoot. I wondered whether I could actually take something quite so large up there.

'Wow, the best blowjob and now anal,' he said. 'This is a dream date.'

I lay on my side to facilitate easier access. Slowly he inched his way up. We took it half-inch by half-inch. Eventually he was there, and happy, as was I. I don't know if it's the naughty factor or the fact that the walls between the anus and vagina are so thin, but a penis in my anus feels almost like double penetration – double pleasure. In this case, it soon became double penetration: I grabbed a vibrator from my bedside drawer and rested it on my clit while Omar explored my ass. I built up to an orgasm over the next ten minutes. Omar waited for me to come, and then, pumping me hard, came up my ass. I felt his cock go soft inside me. Then, just before nodding off, I pulled him out and threw the condom in the basket by my bed. It was like yanking a cork out of a wine bottle – his cock fell on to the mattress with a soft thump, an oddly unsexy sound. Suddenly, it brought us back to earth.

'I can't stay,' Omar said. 'I've got to be up early in the morning. I'm playing tennis with a mate. Sorry, huh?'

'Don't be. I've got a busy day tomorrow myself,' I said. 'Besides, maybe we'll see each other again. I still have to talk to you about that tantric thing.' I was halfway back to dreamland when I heard my front door shut.

I arranged a date for the following day with a cute Irish theatre director named Brendan, another man who contacted me off SwingingHeaven. First, though, I had an appointment with my ex-boyfriend, Jack. We agreed to meet at Primrose Hill Park. It was just around the corner from the Engineer, the fash gastropub where Brendan and I were to meet later. Jack and I spent a couple of hours in the park, some of it playing with his springer spaniel, most of it dissecting Jack's already failing relationship with his girlfriend.

This was the ex-girlfriend for whom he'd left me just a few months earlier. He rehashed the minutiae of his relationship about a dozen times, until the excessive detail and repetition caused me to feel grateful he'd dumped me. I am free! I thought.

There's something liberating about meeting up with a recent ex and feeling nothing. It's almost empowering to realise that, after such intimacy and love and yin-yang harmony, the strings no longer are attached to your groin and heart. Jack had the blues, but I felt happy. I was wearing a pale-blue V-neck sleeveless Ghost dress that clung to my body and accentuated my curves, plus a pair of blue denim wedge high-heeled sandals that gave my calves a boost. My hair still held the becoming bounce and shape the hairdresser had concocted a couple of days earlier. I'd put on a little make-up, too, wanting to both impress Jack and also look good for the man who came after him.

Eventually, it came time to leave Jack to meet Brendan. I was starting to get excited, having half-fantasised about my Irish hottie, half-listened to Jack's sob story. I looked at my watch.

'Look, Jack, I hate to cut you short, but we'd better make a move,' I said. 'I have to meet this guy in fifteen minutes. You want to walk me to the end of the park?'

'Sure, hon.'

We walked to the edge of Primrose Hill and said goodbye. As I turned the corner on to the street where the pub and Brendan awaited, Jack shouted after me, 'You look great. He's a lucky guy.'

I walked to the Engineer and recognised Brendan immediately. He was standing at the bar drinking a Guinness. Just shy of six feet and a dashing combo of curly dark hair and blue eyes. I thought, Jackpot. He fixed me with a look I found utterly charming as well as flattering, in that I interpreted its meaning as: 'Thank God, she looks like her picture.' He said, 'Hello, Suzanne' in a soft Dublin accent that I found sexy.

'Hello. That'll be a glass of white wine.'

He laughed. Jackpot.

We had dinner, or rather I did. Though in one of our pre-meet conversations I'd said, 'I'll book a table,' he somehow hadn't figured that meant we'd actually be eating. He'd already had his dinner, he said, so, as I ate a warm chicken salad, he drank another Guinness.

We chatted about our careers. He had one play going to Edinburgh and another transferring to the West End soon. He was in negotiations for a feature film. A rising talent on the theatre scene, I thought. I wonder what else I can make rise. I looked at him over our table, and began picturing the two of us together. He was very serious, very focused on his work. I wondered if he had thirty-eight-year-old-man Syndrome.

I have an address book full of men in their late thirties, all suffering with the same ailment. They're all men heading for forty, on the fast track and obsessed with achieving their professional goals before the end of their fourth decade. They are all pretty much the same – workaholics, unmarried and extremely ambitious. If they haven't found the love of their life by the time they're thirty-eight, they rationalise; love can wait another few years until they've made their mark. These men are impossible to see regularly – always too busy.

Too busy, that is, until their hormones kick in and they suddenly find themselves horny. That's when they ring me. I can almost schedule their booty calls on my calendar. After the first date, they'll ring me two months later. Then two months after that. Eight weeks is about how long they can go without getting laid.

'You're joking, girl, if you think these guys don't see anyone else but you,' said Pat.

'You're deluded, Suzanne,' said Bernadette.

I'm not so sure I am. I've learnt to spot 38-year-old-man Syndrome from the first five minutes of the very first date, and, after relegating the men to their category, it works for me. Usually, I don't want to see these guys any more frequently than they want to see me.

Brendan, I quickly learnt, fit the profile. 'I'm postponing a relationship for the time being,' he said. Seemed an odd thing to admit on a first date, even to someone he met off SwingingHeaven. Doesn't mean you can't be an occasional tantric partner, I thought.

'Surely, being surrounded by actresses and wannabes, you have plenty of contenders?' I said.

'I don't date actresses,' he said. 'You have to be careful in my profession. I don't want to end up with some mad thespian who thinks I'm going to be her passport to fame.' He recounted a few tragic tales of woe. 'I have to be taken seriously. It just wouldn't look right to date an actress.'

He was so earnest, so serious. According to his moral code, he would not take advantage of aspiring actresses who might see him as a career move, but he had no problem using a middle-aged woman for sex. That confirmed my diagnosis: thirty-eight-year-old-man Syndrome. It felt a little like having dinner with a student. I felt the urge to pat his head and assure him everything would be all right. As well as the urge to teach him a few facts of life. He must have been the only West End director, straight or gay, who actually used a couch for sitting on.

'Lighten up, Brendan,' I said. 'Life really can be fun, you know.' I thought that, if he'd loosen up a little, he might actually be quite fun. He was cute, a little shy and had a charming smile and those twinkly eyes. I wondered if beneath all the earnestness was an animal.

'I do like to get stoned from time to time,' he said, as if to prove he really knew how to live it up.

'Lucky you,' I said. 'I have a joint at my house – if you're interested.' I'd settled into the idea of our spending the rest of the evening at my place.

'Oh. *Oh*. I hadn't realised that you expected to have sex with me tonight,' he said. 'I thought we were just checking each other out. I wanted to make sure you weren't a nutter.' Brendan told me that he had a playwright friend visiting from Ireland and he had to 'shoot off' by nine p.m. to meet his mate at Camden Town station. 'What about next time we skip dinner and I meet you at your place with a bottle of wine and some really good hash?'

I was disappointed but thought there existed the promise for a future rendezvous. Plus, I still hadn't yet posed the tantric idea. I wondered if he'd be up to it. He liked his hash, at least, and I assumed he liked sex, at least every eight weeks. But what kind of guy thought that, by answering an ad on a swinging site, he'd be going on a real date?

We walked to Camden Town Station together, had a quick snog outside the Tube and arranged to meet up soon. He knew how to kiss: good sign. I drove home that night hoping I hadn't wasted my time – and money, having paid for my salad.

The next weekend I had an appointment with Andy, the 'tantric masseur and stud'. Since our previous date at Rio's, he was my first and only tantric partner. As I discovered after that first time together, he was an expert lover and we had a mind–body connection like none I'd ever experienced with anyone before. Our bodies fitted together – like two pieces of a puzzle, I remember thinking, guiltily, that thought being so unoriginal. And yet, we sure did fit: he could stay hard for hours. For the first time in my life, I experienced the 'waves of pleasure' Jahnet had told me about, almost coming, again and again, until finally building to that well-earned climax. He was sensitive and caring.

Each time we met I would lay two foam mattresses on my sitting-room floor, cover them with an Indian bedspread I'd bought in Goa before my marriage. Andy would take out a massage oil he had specially prepared for me that smelt of ylang ylang, geranium and rose. I'd lie on my stomach and he'd massage my back, easing out the knots in my shoulder and neck before moving down my body. Soon he would be massaging my labia and I would feel myself getting wet. I'd turn over and he would go to work on the rest of me, massaging my breasts, my abdomen, up and down my legs, until finally settling back on my pussy and gently massaging my vagina. Thank you, Jahnet, I'd think.

After such sensitive touch and loving attention, I would be deeply relaxed and more than ready for him. We would fuck for hours, neither of us thinking about coming, just enjoying the waves of pleasure that make tantric sex so unique. When the energy became too great and both of us felt we were plunging towards orgasm, we would stop. Then we'd settle into the scissor position, our legs entwined, Andy inside me. We would stay in this position for twenty or thirty minutes, perfectly still.

'You must let yourself go,' Jahnet had instructed, and with Andy and tantric it was easy to comply. I would be transported to an otherworldly place where all that mattered was rhythm and pace and all I felt were endorphins and pleasure. Closeness, too – it was dreamlike, this union of two bodies. In a sense, the tantric goal of pleasure coupled with detachment meant it had something in common with swinging clubs and anonymous sex. It certainly wasn't about love in either case. But in swinging clubs I got off on getting men off. It wasn't about my pleasure; it was about the excitement I got from turning on so many men and making them come. It was vampiric, sucking up male energy. Tantric is the opposite: the focus is firmly on me. In tantric sex, men withhold their orgasm in order to please the woman they are with, connecting solely with them, following their rhythm. Partners combine their energies so that both reach the same peaks at the same time – the circle of energy, not just the usual orgasmic payoff.

Jahnet had taught me enough to get started. Now, practising concepts explored in some books on tantric sex I'd bought, I felt I was making progress with my homework. I had one partner; I needed another two. If I found my three tantric partners, I believed, I could carry on this way for a very long time.

Keeping detached – Jahnet's other homework assignment, along with finding three tantric partners – was easy when I didn't have an intellectual connection with my tantric partner. And I didn't have much to say to Andy – we had very little in common, led very different lives and there was a ten year age gap – so I had no desire to speak to him or see him in between our meetings.

'I know we're supposed to be detached,' he said once, 'but sometimes I just want to talk to you.' He confessed that sometimes he longed for me, but that he was trying to get beyond that. Visualisation exercises apparently helped. 'I just breathe through the feelings of wanting to be with you. I think it's working.'

I didn't know what to say to my sexy tantric hippy hottie. 'I'm sorry, Andy. You knew the rules when we met. I just want a tantric partner once a month, and in between our meetings there's to be no communication,' I said. Then I used my trump card: 'That's Jahnet's homework.'

I thought about what Jahnet had said: 'It may take a dozen men, maybe more, before you find your three.' I wondered if at some point in my journey Andy might have to go, but for now he was just homework.

The day before one of Andy's visits, my son Martin and I were making my bed. He and Alfred had their bags packed by the front door, ready for the car ride that would take them to another weekend with their father.

'Can you help me turn the mattress, honey?' I asked. The mattress was a monster, impossible to move alone, and even with another body helping me I figured it would probably prove impossible to budge. After fifteen years of use and abuse – a cliché phrase that, in this case, was wholly appropriate because all too true – it had become weighted down with my and other people's sweat and smegma and blood and history. The stuffing was so tightly compressed now, I could hardly move the mattress an inch even when changing the sheets.

Martin and I stood on the edge of the bed, using the force of our combined body weights and muscles to lift the mattress off the base. We managed to raise it up a half-metre, just enough to notice a massive rip on the underside. The calico cover had split. Stuffing was spilling out from between the raw edges of the tear, little pieces snowing down on to the base.

'Mum, I think it's time you got a new mattress.'

14. THE NEAR MISS

I met Karume at the launch party of Charing X, advertised as being the world's first erotic art gallery, on Charing Cross Road. I had bagged an invitation through a friend of a friend and invited Oliver along, who after our first liaison in Soho House had become a regular fuck buddy. We had a regular Wednesday-night date, watching *Desperate Housewives* and fucking during the commercial breaks.

When we arrived at the gallery it was packed with media trendies – a few girls dressed in rubber and leather; some burlesque chicks wearing nipple tassles, stockings and suspenders; a sprinkling of glamour models popping out of their bikinis. I wore a 1940s brown-and-green patterned-lace dress over skin and a pair of high Buddhahood sandals.

The gallery was on four floors in a former sex shop. The owners had stripped out the vibrators and porn and painted the walls white, leaving the adult bookstore on the ground floor, presumably for the smut to pay the rent if the art didn't. Looking at the stuff on the walls, I concluded they'd made the right move. I'd seen most of what they were selling countless times before, in the bedrooms of some of my middle-class conquests and even in framing-shop windows in respectable neighbourhoods. The new Helmut Newtons weren't so different from the old Helmut Newtons, Bob Carlos Clarke's obsessive studies of perfect female bodies were more sterile than sexy, the giant glass dildos attached to fox tails and expensive price tags were so thirty years ago. But then this was an art crowd, not an erotic crowd. The fetish girls were familiar faces from other events and most of the other people in the room hadn't made much of an effort – the T-shirt-and-jeans boys and the suits mixed with the bikinis and pasties girls – so at best people exuded cute but not sex. Good thing this is just a pit stop, I found myself thinking. In an hour I was meeting my girlfriend Hannah at Flash Monkey, a party at the Café de Paris around the corner.

Oliver and I looked around the gallery a bit, then pushed our way to the bar to pick up a couple of drinks. 'I'm out of here in ten minutes,' I said. 'I've got a real party to go to.'

That's when Oliver spotted a friend at the top of the stairs. 'Come with me, Suzanne. You should meet Karume. He's an artist.'

We walked up to the first floor and Oliver introduced me to a tall good-looking man with dark-brown skin the colour of a Belgian truffle. Karume had a resonant voice and diamond-sharp enunciation, and he spoke with an accent I couldn't place. Originally from Kenya, I learnt, he had lived in the States as a kid, grown up in Africa, and left Nairobi for London a few years earlier. He was wearing his unique inter-pretation of a cyclist's uniform – a black sweater, black longjohns under three-quarter-length nylon elasticated trousers and red cycling shoes. His clothes were so inappropriate for an art-gallery event it was hard to tell if it was his outfit or his beauty that drew people's attention, ladies and gents alike. His trousers were so tight the sizeable bulge at his crotch caught my eye. Karume noticed me noticing, so I pretended my focus was elsewhere. I saw a Ferrari logo on his footwear – phew, something to talk about. 'Nice trainers,' I said.

'Ferrari, as you can see. I always wanted to own a Ferrari,' he said. He had a crooked smile that turned up at one end. 'I like to imagine that one day I'll have the trainers *and* the car.'

'We all live in hope, man,' I said. 'Me included.' I was hoping he'd stick around. I liked his high cheekbones, his aquiline nose, his big white teeth and dark eyes and long black eyelashes. His shoulders were wide and his hips narrow, so his torso tapered into a swashbuckler's T. His straight hair fell to his shoulders, girl length, but, on Karume, very masculine. I noticed that his brown lower lip was spotted with tiny pink patches. The lack of pigmentation was distracting but gave him an unusual look. I liked that. Plenty of men are generically attractive; it's what's different about a man that makes him sexy.

'What do you think of the art?' he asked.

'Not much,' I said. 'I've seen a lot of this before. I don't know how they're going to make enough money to keep four floors in the West End. Surely, you can buy most of this stuff on the web.'

'What about the people? Can't find them on the web, can you?'

If you only knew how many men I've found on the web, I thought. I ignored the latter question and answered the former. 'The people here? I wouldn't be surprised if most of them don't even have sex. What's erotic about them? They're as sterile as the gallery walls. Even their costumes are generic.'

'Well, there's the corset,' said Karume. 'That's erotic, I think. Did you see it? Made from human bone.'

I told him I'd seen many things in my life but a human-bone corset was not one of them.

'C'mon, I'll show you.'

I followed him to a mannequin wearing a corset made of bone, hair and fabric and held together by embossed-silver fasteners. It was very tiny and looked not just unwearable but downright punishing – far too small and fragile for a human being, but quite beautiful as a piece of sculpture.

'If I had the money, I'd buy it,' said Karume. 'Not to wear – don't get any ideas, my lady. It's definitely the best piece here, don't you think?' It was unusual, a real one-off, unlike so much else in the gallery. We circled the mannequin, admiring its handiwork and the intricacy and originality of the design. 'You like this thing but say you're unimpressed with the rest of the stuff here,' said Karume. 'What *do* you find erotic, then? Are you turned on by the restraints on the corset or something?'

'Good question,' I said. 'Really, it's the smallest things that turn me on.' I started laughing. Given the men I'd been with and what kept them in my memories, the words 'erotic' and 'small' weren't typically paired. 'A look, a gesture ...'

Oliver, the odd-man-out in this three-way, had wandered off, leaving Karume and me alone. I told Karume about the time I was in a naturist club, standing at a mirror drying my hair, when I caught a naked man watching me, wanking. 'I only caught a glimpse of him, but the look we exchanged fuelled my fantasies for months.'

'A naturist club.' Karume spoke slowly, staring ahead as if picturing something in his mind. Dirty thoughts and deeds involving me, I hoped. Instead, he said, 'I don't think that I could go to a place like that.'

'Who knows? You might like it.'

'I'm not sure I would want everyone to see ... everything.' I couldn't tell if he was being judgemental or prudish. Then he explained, 'I have a very unique cock, you know.'

I'd just met Karume and already we were talking sex. He was no prude. That's a key criterion in a man. 'Really? Unique?' I said, wondering what made his cock so special.

'Yes,' he said. 'Very.' He didn't elaborate. I imagined something so long it hung down to his knees. We stayed by the corset pretending to look at the little torture device, though in our thoughts we'd already moved beyond it. Neither of us spoke for a few minutes.

I broke the silence. 'Well, you must show me your unique cock. There must be a bathroom in this place somewhere.'

'I can't show you *now*,' he said. He seemed alarmed, as if he hadn't considered that, in telling me about his unique cock, I might actually want to see it. 'You'll just have to wait,' he said. 'Why don't you give me your number?'

'No. I don't give out my number anymore,' I said. 'You give me yours and, if I want to speak to you, I'll ring.' I pegged Karume as a numbers collector. He probably had an address book full of women's numbers, most of them never dialled, and I didn't want to risk losing him. There was more likelihood we'd meet again if I had his contact info. He laughed and passed me his number.

I found Karume easy to talk to. He reminded me of Daniel, who always attracted a circle of girls whenever we went out. I didn't imagine Karume found it hard to meet women, either – he was attractive, charming and friendly, and he had a cool job. He told me he taught art at a south London university. I ticked the boxes in my head: good-looking, funny, fit, sexy, employed. What a catch.

Karume walked me to Flash Monkey, falling behind a few feet as we made our way. 'I like the rear view,' he said, laughing.

I liked his frisky attitude. When we got to the door I kissed him on both cheeks. 'Bye,' I said, and went inside to meet Hannah.

I called Karume later that night while driving home. It was one in the morning. 'What are you doing?' I asked.

He was on a bus, also going home for the night. 'Should I turn around?'

I was tempted to say yes, but filed him under 'future playmate' instead. 'No, it's too late. But you have my number now, so give me a ring sometime.'

I assumed he would. I felt we had truly connected. He was originally from another country, like me; in his forties, like me; and had been married, like me. His mum had been a school teacher, just like mine. And as he'd lived in the States as a kid before moving back to Kenya as a teenager, like me he had grown up watching *Captain Kangaroo* and *Mr Rogers'*

Neighborhood on the TV. We even knew the lyrics to the same commercials. So I was surprised when a week later Karume still hadn't called. I wondered if the connection I'd felt had just been a one-way phenomenon after all. Oh, well. There are others, I thought, but, figuring it was worth another shot, I left a message on his mobile.

'I'm free next Friday, Mr Unusual Cock, if you want to meet up.'

Again, no return call, so a few days later I booked a date with Anthony, my hot cop, instead. On Wednesday, Karume rang. 'Still free on Friday?'

'Nope, Karume. Afraid that slot is now filled.' Even if Anthony weren't on the agenda, I would have said the same thing. I didn't want Karume thinking me so desperate I'd drop everything for him, last minute. Somehow, his much-delayed return call didn't seem all that different in spirit from the impromptu calls I used to get back in my twenties from the three a.m. boys. I was too old for this. When it came to last-minute booty calls, I'd learnt to take on the role of initiator. 'I don't know when I'm free next,' I continued. 'I'll ring you sometime and let you know.'

'Oh. OK,' Karume said. He sounded disappointed, and I was glad. 'I guess next time I should react a bit quicker.'

'That would be my advice,' I said. 'My slots fill up quickly.'

'Sure seems that way.'

After the weekend I rang Karume. 'I'm going to be at Soho House tonight for a meeting. Why don't you swing by after ten and join me?'

Karume turned up on time, once again in tight biking gear, and walked into the Circle Bar. He smiled when he saw me and came to the table. I was just finishing up discussing a business project with my friend Jonathan. 'Ah, here's my date,' I said, and made the introductions. Jonathan ordered a round of drinks, so it was another hour before Karume and I were alone together. It was now eleven on a Monday night. I had work the next day. I turned to Karume and said, 'Shall we go back to mine?'

'Lead the way.'

Karume threw his bike in the back of my cabriolet and I apologised for keeping him waiting. 'I thought I'd made it clear that you were a date,' I said. 'I really wanted to be alone with you.' That seemed to please him.

Back in my kitchen, I poured two glasses of wine and passed Karume a bag of grass. He rolled a joint, lit it and passed it to me. I handed the joint back to him, then sat on Karume's lap and kissed him. We kissed for a very long time – another good sign, because, to me, kissing the right man can be foreplay, and too many men just want to get to business. His tongue was gentle and probing, circling around my own, licking my lips. I put a hand on his pants, felt his cock stiffen and gently rubbed it. His cock pushed against the fabric of his cyclist's trousers. When we moved apart finally, we laughed, half-stoned, half-embarrassed by the sudden intensity.

'It's getting late, and I have to get up early tomorrow,' I said, smirking. 'Want to go to bed?'

He followed me upstairs to the bedroom. We removed our tops en route. As Karume took off his shirt, I could see he had a tasty body. His perfect T-shape had impressed me the night we met; now I was impressed by his perfect six-pack. In the bedroom, when he removed his pants, I saw how his muscular shoulders and back tapered down to a firm round bottom. He had the legs of a cyclist – muscular thighs, meaty calves. Then I saw his cock. Karume was right – it was unique. The lack of pigmentation that I'd noticed on his lips had similarly affected other parts of his body. His elbows were pink. One nipple was pink. The head of his thick eight-inch cock was pink as well, in sharp contrast to the rest of it. It was unlike any cock I'd ever seen: not the largest or thickest, but big enough to satisfy a size queen and a visual novelty besides.

'Suck my cock,' he said.

I sat on the edge of my bed, took his cock in my mouth and watched the brown shaft get harder and longer. I wanted to worship that cock, linger over the head with my tongue, feel its size fill my mouth and throat.

Karume cupped the back of my head in his hands, willing me to take him further down my throat. I opened my mouth wider to allow his cock to penetrate, relaxing the back of my throat to accommodate him. He held his cock there for a moment. I slid back until my lips were enveloping the tip. I used my saliva to glide my hand up and down the shaft.

'That … feels … fan … tastic,' he said.

I rubbed my clit along Karume's thigh while sucking him off. I licked and sucked and caressed his cock with my mouth and hands until I was dripping. I felt the energy from his body course through my own, his pleasure mirroring my own. As his cock hardened and softened, as his excitement grew and subsided, so did my own excitement.

Finally, when I couldn't stand the anticipation any longer, I straddled him. He was as hard as a rolling pin. I rode his cock, teasing the head with my pussy and grinding on his hips, hoping he would not go soft while I was on top, as many men I've been with tended to do. Happily, with Karume that was not a problem. Even as I rested, motionless, when there was no friction, he remained rock-hard inside me. This was a rare gift; many men need the friction and constant movement to stay hard. I didn't want to come quickly and, with Jahnet's tantric lessons in mind, was happy to have found a man equally willing to go slow. I wanted to savour the feeling of having Karume inside me – and touch his body, kiss his lips, look into his eyes. Ah, Jahnet, I thought, you did say there were men out there for me. This sure wasn't the usual fuck-buddy scenario.

Too often, it is tempting to think of a sex partner as a dildo attached to a body. With Karume I felt like our life energies travelled through one and into the other, a pleasure cycle of sexual and human connectedness. I felt the endorphins switch on inside my body. I was almost too excited, too stimulated, to orgasm. Every few minutes we'd stop and lie next to each other on my bed, holding hands, touching each other's body, kissing – relaxing and enjoying being together.

We worked well as a pair. Karume enjoyed being dominant, and to my surprise I enjoyed letting him lead; it was comfortable being a more passive partner than usual. After lying together during one of our rest periods, he said, 'Roll on to your stomach.' I did as commanded. 'Bend your leg.' I bent my right leg. Then he pushed my thigh up towards my chest and thrust deeply into me from behind. I felt him push back, arching his back, as he drove his full length into me. He hit the roof of my vagina. It was almost painful, but I enjoyed the discomfort and the feeling of being taken so roughly. He grabbed my hips with one hand and pulled me into him, while pushing his thumb into my mouth with his free hand. 'Suck this,' he said. I complied. He fucked me hard for ten punishing minutes, then flipped me over again, lay on top of my body, caressed my breasts and kissed me.

'Please lick my pussy,' I begged.

'No.'

I was surprised that someone so sexual and so responsive to his partner would deny this request. 'You're going to have to learn to wait,' he said. 'It's good for you.'

I was relieved Karume didn't find the idea of oral sex repulsive, and, bizarrely, I was turned on by his blunt refusal. I decided to let Karume be the boss when we fucked. I cleared my dirty mind of all sex plans – no thoughts of what to do next, of which position to take – and went on a sexual holiday, accepting each new adventure as it came my way. I felt a bit like a human blow-up sex doll, passively doing as I was told. I was Karume's porn-fantasy woman, always complying, never resisting. And it was great.

Karume fucked me for three hours that night. We both came while I was riding his cock, on top, as at the beginning of the night. After we washed up, I saw that the summer sun was beginning to rise. I knew I'd be getting up for work soon, yet didn't feel any great urge to sleep. I enjoyed resting my head on Karume's shoulder, wrapping my arms around him, cuddling in the middle of my big bed – so relaxed, so still, so quiet. Even though it was our first night together, I felt at peace with Karume. I sensed I'd found a kindred spirit, not just a great lay. We both knew it was more than a one-night stand.

The next time I invited Karume to spend the night, even though the kids were away at American Camp, I made sure it was a weekend. I wanted to concentrate on the sex, not be distracted by a clock ticking towards the next work day. I cooked him dinner while he retrieved two martini glasses from a cabinet and mixed a drink called a Golden Angel. 'I invented this for you,' he said. 'I know how you Americans like your orange juice and, with a little apple juice and a lot of Russian vodka, I think you'll find it magnificent – just like you: magnificent.'

The cocktail became our tradition, a kind of liquid foreplay that always led to a long night in bed. That second night together, we fucked for four hours. Once again Karume was impressively tantric and masterful – taking his time, seemingly indifferent to his own orgasm. Over breakfast the following morning, I told him about Jahnet and my tantric lessons. 'She wants me to find three tantric partners. I already have one, but I need another two. Would you like to be one of them and practise tantric with me?'

'Tantric?' he said. 'That's funny. My last partner and I were really into that.' He said he once went two weeks without coming, despite fucking every night. It was to conserve his male energy, he explained; the more he waited to come, the more alert his senses seemed to become. 'But why three partners?' he continued. 'Wouldn't you prefer to have just one? A master? My name means "master" in Kenyan, you know. This is a role I was born to play.'

'Jahnet says I'm not ready for a boyfriend, that it's too soon to settle down with any one man.'

'Well, I'm a one-woman man,' Karume said, frowning. He sounded like he meant it.

I contemplated what he was telling me. 'You mean you want an exclusive thing? With me?'

He arched his eyebrows and smirked. I replayed highlights of our two nights together in my head. I thought about his going two weeks without coming, devoting his male energy, like a true tantric master, to his partner's pleasure. That sold me. 'Well, I suppose I could bend the rules.'

He laughed. 'I'd like that. Let's see how it goes.'

Karume and I started seeing each other regularly soon afterwards. He'd leave sweet love notes on my pillow in the morning. And our evening Golden Angels became a bonding potion. As for the sex, it continued to be exceptional. Very quickly I found myself growing fonder and fonder of Karume and thinking about him when he wasn't around. And, when he was around, I enjoyed seeing how comfortable he was with my boys. They took to him immediately. He treated them like friends, not like children.

I soon discovered that, although Karume often left little love notes on my pillow, he wasn't the best communicator, so it was hard to predict when I'd see him next. Just scheduling get-togethers was a frustration from the start. His phone always seemed to be switched off. 'I can never get a signal,' he said. 'I can't be bothered.'

Karume and I soon settled into a pattern. Three or four nights a week he would stay over at my place and, once he was at the house, I knew he'd be there for a few days and I wouldn't have to think about chasing him down. But, rather than stay in for the evening, he would go cycling along the Embankment after the boys went to bed. He would not return until after midnight. In the first weeks under this arrangement, I slept very little. Still, I looked forward to his returning and joining me in bed, because I loved having him inside me. His cock filled me up. And his body and mine fitted perfectly – he was neither so tiny that I'd overwhelm him nor so bulky that he'd overwhelm me. He turned me on, my dappled lover. And he knew how to make me come.

At first I thought my biggest problem would be preventing myself from coming too soon. We were tantric partners, after all; our spiritual connection came first; the orgasm was supposed to be secondary. But sex with Karume was so good I had to force myself not to come. A few weeks into our arrangement, however, Karume's late-night wake-up calls began taking their toll. I found it disappointing not being able to enjoy his company before going to bed. But the real complication was that, the morning after a marathon sex session, I would be exhausted when I woke to take my boys to school. The pleasantly groggy afterglow of our first weeks together soon became an unwelcome energy drain. But I put up with it. He was the master.

Karume's schedule quickly changed my clock. I would wake up after midnight and wonder where my lover was. Some nights he didn't return at all, explaining, when I called the next day, that he'd stayed in Brixton. Or in Ladbroke Grove. Or with a friend. He seemed to have no set residence. When I asked about Brixton, he said he had a friend there who let him stay in a spare room in exchange for running errands and performing maintenance tasks on the property. I imagined a wealthy elderly woman, tiny and weak and grateful for a guy's help with the chores. I never met her, nor did I see his room in her house. Never saw his flat in Ladbroke Grove either. 'I'm doing it up real nice, Suzanne,' he said, 'but it's an unspeakable mess at the moment, really just a building site.' He promised to have me over for a romantic candlelit dinner when it was finished.

I knew little of his life beyond the experiences we shared when we were together. When we had sex, he pounded any doubts out of my mind, at least temporarily. Karume was a tantric master, just as he'd boasted at our first meeting, and we had fun fucking and taking wagers on how many days he could go without coming. He had profound stores of energy and always stayed hard for hours. Despite sleeping very little – three hours per night was typical for him – he always looked great the next morning. I did not. Eventually, Karume's odd hours, plus the hours spent fucking rather than sleeping, frayed me. If I don't have seven hours' sleep, I'm knackered; if I have a couple of rough nights like that in a row, I'm destroyed. So, though I loved the sex, I put a moratorium on sleeplessness. 'All this no sleep is really doing my head in,' I told him a couple of months after I'd begun feeling we were a real couple. 'I love the sex, love having you here, but I love my sleep, too. You can't keep coming back at one or two in the morning, Karume.' I told him that, if he couldn't make it home by eleven, he should spend the night elsewhere.

We saw each other less frequently thereafter, as, apparently, he couldn't seem to make it back by curfew. It didn't matter to me. We had a great connection, and I appreciated catching up on my sleep on those nights off. I got used to him just turning up when he felt like it. He seemed increasingly comfortable with the arrangement as well, gradually moving more of his things into the house. Every week I found a new pile of his clothes in my wardrobe or a new bag in the hallway. I didn't protest because, when he was there, he was great with my boys and good to me. They really liked him, and I liked the adult company. Karume was a good cook, too, and like Daniel would fix the boys after-school snacks before I got home and do the laundry and tend the garden.

One day when I returned home from work I found him washing the kitchen floor.

'What are you doing?' I said. 'Didn't Gabriela come today?' Gabriela was my Slovakian cleaner. A no-show one week out of every four, she wasn't very dependable. She wasn't an exceptional cleaner, either, but she wasn't so bad that replacing her was worth the effort. Besides, she was the one person with whom my Slovakian au pair, adorable Josef, could really communicate.

'Yes, she came today,' said Karume, 'and mostly sat around drinking coffee and chatting with friends on her mobile. She's a useless cow.'

I suggested that next time he politely tell her to get back to work.

'It's not really my place, Suzanne. You should just get a new cleaner. Or let me do it.' I thought he was joking. He wasn't.

'I am *not* letting you clean my house. Do you know how hard it is to find a decent cleaner in London? I've been through five in five years. And, when you tire of me, master, I've lost both my lover *and* my cleaner. Forget it.'

So Karume continued to pick up after the maid and watch over my boys and fuck me and become a part-time husband. And a full-time financial drain as well. He never had any money and, I soon discovered, this was his lifestyle, not a phase. He'd said he was a guest art lecturer, but I later learnt that gig ended three months before we met. He said buyers and gallery owners showed interest in his work, yet he never showed me his art; I never saw him creating art; and the art sales and exhibitions never came to pass. He said he had worked as a sound engineer but that there wasn't much work at the studios any more. This surprised me, given London's lively music scene, but I figured he knew the production end of the industry better than me. He said he was an aspiring writer, too. He once showed me the outline for a book he wanted to write, but the project never got past the outline stage.

Ultimately, it was lots of ideas but not lots of money. I didn't know how he paid for his life in London. Certainly, he never carried any money with him. He never took me out, never brought a bottle of wine to the house, never offered to put petrol in the car, never picked up the tab in restaurants. I realised there were many 'nevers' attached to any thoughts related to Karume and his finances. And, after enduring Daniel's destitution for more than two years and going into debt to subsidise him, I was wary of hitching my tits to another impoverished guy.

All signs pointed to the exit. Yet I was always horny around Karume. And, when we got into bed at night, I wanted to feel him inside me, to suck his beautiful brown cock. I no longer needed to conjure sexual fantasies in order to come. It was just me and Karume and the thought of his big hard cock inside one of my orifices – that was enough to get me there. I'd given plenty of blowjobs before, fucked many dozens of men, but not since Frank had I felt such intensity of emotion and energy with a sexual partner. Just being around Karume made me feel happy and relaxed and, after a long day at the office and an evening spent looking after my two boys, it was a battery recharge to open my mouth and legs and let someone take control in bed.

One Friday night a few months after we met, Karume said he needed to go to a meeting in Waterloo for a couple of hours. 'I have to wrap up some business with a woman who wants to talk about my sound installation,' he said. 'She wants to bring it to Paris.' We had been drinking Golden Angel martinis, so this came as a surprise. I had assumed his next destination was my bed.

'I'll be back as soon as I can,' he said. 'The second one is on me.'

I smiled at the joke. We were at my place, drinking my vodka.

Karume put on his cycling gear and went outside. He returned a minute later, saying his lock had jammed and his bike was chained to my railings. 'Take Alfred's bike,' I said. 'He's your co-dependent anyway.' Karume had been using my son's mobile for weeks, as Alfred never used it and Karume's own had run out of credit.

'I'll be back in a couple of hours – promise,' he said. 'I want to spend the weekend fucking you sore. Starting tonight.'

'Sounds naughty,' I said. 'Hurry back.' It was eleven p.m. Factoring in the trip across town and back, I figured it would be two a.m. before I saw Karume again. I took a hot relaxing bath in preparation for the long night ahead.

By noon the next day Karume still hadn't turned up. I began worrying that something might have happened to him. I rang the A&E departments at St Thomas' and the Royal Free but he wasn't in either. Then I remembered Karume's discarded mobile phone was still in my house. I hoped I'd find someone on his call list who might know where he was. There was a message in his inbox from the night before, so I listened to that first. It was from a woman named Cheryl, telling Karume when to meet her at the Social in Waterloo. He'd never mentioned a Cheryl before. I rang Cheryl's number and went straight into her answer machine.

'This is Suzanne, Karume's girlfriend,' I said. 'I just wanted to know when you saw him last. He didn't come home last night and I'm just making sure he's OK.'

I returned to the call list. There had been four calls, one after another, from someone named Rula – another unfamiliar name. I rang the number and a woman with a Scandanavian accent answered the phone. 'He came by in someone's car on Thursday to pick up some of his stuff,' she said. 'Sorry, who is this?'

'Suzanne,' I said. 'Karume's girlfriend.'

'*Girlfriend*?' She laughed. 'How weird. He's been trying to get back with *me* for the past three months, pestering me to take him back.'

'But ...' There was no point in forming sentences.

'Anyway, he finally came by and got his stuff, because I ended it,' she continued. 'I got sick of his always playing around. For good reason, as you can imagine. Sorry, Susan.'

'*Suzanne.*'

I felt like an idiot. On Thursday night I'd gone to Liverpool with a colleague to help with a screening for a movie I was publicising. Karume must have taken my car while I was gone and driven to Rula's. He didn't have a licence or insurance. But he did have an alibi. When I returned home on Friday morning, he had asked if I'd noticed he'd moved my car. 'I saw a space right in front of the house and thought I'd move the car closer for you.'

I had noticed more of his clothes hanging in my wardrobe later that afternoon ('I spend half the week here, so it seemed to make sense'), as well as a new stereo ('I thought of you when I picked this up; thought maybe you could use it somewhere') and more clothes in bags in the basement ('In case the weather changes'). My trip, I now realised, had given him the opportunity to retrieve his things from Rula's and store them at what I'd come to think of as 'our' place.

Rula and I compared schedules and stories and alibis. We discovered we each saw him on the days the other didn't, such as the previous Tuesday, when he'd stayed at Rula's but told me he was working on his flat. Like me, Rula had never seen it. Like me, she had been promised a romantic candlelit dinner when the rehab on the flat was complete.

'OK,' she said, 'he was with me on Tuesday. Was he with you on Wednesday?'

'Yeah. We stayed in, had dinner at home.'

'Prick. He told me he was staying with his agent. What was I thinking? Who stays with their agent? They sell your stuff; they don't put you up for the night. I had a feeling someone was in the background.'

'We're both idiots,' I said.

'Let me guess. He left little love notes on your pillow all the time?' She described the paper he wrote notes on; it came from my kitchen pad.

'Prick' I said. 'So tell me: you live in Brixton, right?'

She did.

I packed his stuff in bags and put everything outside my door. Then I phoned Anthony, who came round, changed my locks and, using his stern policeman voice, rang Karume to tell him his bags were on the street and demand they be collected within the hour.

'Cheers, Anthony,' I said.

'I don't want to get in the middle of this, Suzanne, and I realise you're upset, but all the guy did was cheat, right? It's not actually a crime.'

To me, deceiving me was the crime. Honesty, like big cocks, is high on my list.

Anthony left after making sure Karume picked up his things without causing a scene. Then I called Pat to have a bitch.

'Why is everyone so judgemental about my lifestyle, about my fucking so many guys? I'm honest, at least. We all know the score. No one gets conned. It's simple.' Then I started crying. 'Karume lied to me.'

'He's a complete fucker,' she said, adding that she'd never liked him anyway. 'That's why I haven't been ringing you, actually. I'm glad he's gone.'

I'd been dumped before by girlfriends who disapproved of my choice in men or because they feared my promiscuous behaviour reflected badly on them. I'd got used to the negative comments.

'I don't get it,' I continued. 'I'd asked him if he wanted to be one of my tantric guys and just get together once in a while. He could have seen me *and* kept his other girlfriend. Instead, he made me drop my harem while keeping his own. Bastard!'

'It may sound simple to you, Suzanne,' she said. 'But most guys don't want to be part of a harem. It's the old double standard.'

While I raged over his deception, I pondered whether I still loved the guy. I loved his cooking, loved having a man around for the kids, loved the romantic cocktail hours. As for the man himself, well, Karume played tennis with my boys every Saturday morning and video games with them most evenings, and he was often around to help them with the homework. I knew that money was always going to be a problem, as it had been with Daniel, but he had seemed an improvement over Daniel, somehow, if only because he didn't fall asleep in front of the telly every night. Special bonus: he didn't have addiction problems. And he could fuck for Britain.

I wasn't sure I wanted to knock Karume out of my life forever, but I knew I didn't want a boyfriend whom I couldn't trust. So, as with Jack and Oliver, I recompartmentalised. A week after I changed the locks on the doors, I found myself driving through Karume's neighbourhood while returning home after cocktails at the Electric with Hannah. He was now living in a spare room in a flat in Lancaster Gate.

I rang his mobile. 'Hi, Karume,' I said. 'I'm just around the corner. Fancy a nightcap?'

'I'll be right down,' he said. 'I want to talk to you.'

'I'm really sorry,' he said as he got in the car. 'I was dumb.'

'Yes, you were,' I said. 'You could have kept Rula *and* me. That's what I don't get. I've got to be the most open-minded woman on the planet, and still you played me.'

'Yeah, I know,' he agreed. 'Listen, I'd really like to make it up to you. I was wondering, do you still have that useless cleaner?'

'No. I took your advice and sacked her – and replaced her with a klepto. Last time the new one cleaned the house, my topaz earrings went home with her.'

'Let *me* clean your house,' he said.

'Are you serious?'

'Yes, I'm serious,' he said. 'You know I like cleaning, and those girls only work a couple of hours.'

'And charge me for six,' I said. 'Well, if you're serious, it's cool with me – if you're talking about doing it every week, like a regular job. I'm not interested in a one-off atonement cleaning job.'

Finding a boyfriend is easy, but scoring a top cleaner is not. Particularly one with benefits, who'll stay at the house after going off duty and, in exchange for dinner and a Golden Angel martini, help me dirty up my bed. I drove home – with Karume – a content woman.

I phoned up Jahnet and told her about Karume.

'Now you have to start all over again, Suzanne,' she said. 'Again. This is the second time you've strayed from the path. Find your three tantric lovers, dear. Three! And no boyfriends!'

'Well, Karume was a tantric lover,' I protested.

'And a boyfriend as well,' she scolded. 'You disobeyed me, going out with those silly men. No boyfriends. Now you have to start all over again.'

She was right. I didn't need a boyfriend. I had fallen into a relationship with Karume even though I knew he wasn't

Mr Right – he wasn't even Mr Almost. I should have stuck to my homework of finding three tantric partners.

I grabbed my mobile and scrolled the names of erstwhile funboys. After trying and failing at a monogamous setup with Jack, I'd learned my lesson and not deleted anyone's number despite taking up with Karume. I hadn't told any of my guys I'd exited the scene; I just stopped calling and responding to messages.

My first call was to Tantric Andy.

'So glad to hear from you, Suzanne,' he said. 'I've missed you. I'd given up hope I'd ever find such a perfect pussy again.'

Now I just needed two more willing guys. I typed a brief message to the contenders: I'M AROUND THIS WEEKEND. ARE YOU FREE? IT WOULD BE NICE TO SEE YOU. Then I plugged into the address line the names of my favourite playmates, and hit Send.

I got wet just thinking about the auditions ahead and wondered if Jahnet would consider that a good thing. Tantric is about spending time with someone purely for the sake of pleasure, so, in essence, my funboys were all tantric partners in training – seekers of pleasure who were generous with their bodies and open to new ways of thinking. I'd never get an 'A' in my tantric class, but maybe a 'B+' was within sight. In line with Jahnet's criteria, my funboys would never be boyfriends; we saw each other just on weekends and rarely more than once a month; and our sessions were devoted to mutual pleasure and nothing more.

Within a minute of sending the text message, my phone lit up.

WELCOME BACK. I'D LOVE TO SEE YOU. LET'S MEET UP. It was from Greg. Tall blond athletic marathon-fuck, Big Cock London Greg.

I smiled. I was back on the market. And it felt good.